Th

MW01290240

Relationship Lessons From The Garden of Eden

By David A. Burrus

Please note that The David Burrus Companies publishing
style capitalizes certain pronouns in scripture that refer to
Father, Son and Holy Spirit, and may differ from some Bible
publisher's styles.

Editing by Michelle G. Cameron:
MichelleGCameron@gmail.com

For more information email us at:
admin@davidaburrus.com

Find us on the world wide web:
www.davidaburrus.com

Follow David on Twitter, Periscope and Instagram:
@DavidABurrus

Follow David on Facebook:
@DavidABurrusOfficial

Books By David A. Burrus

The Kingdom Driven Entrepreneur's
Guide to Extraordinary Leadership

Think On These Things: A Devotional for
Faith Enrichment

The Fire Starter Effect: Activating
The Power of Covenant

The Pursuit of Purpose

Foreword

The Blueprint: Relationship Lessons From The Garden of Eden presents an awesome body of work that will add immediate value to its readers. David Burrus takes a practical approach in providing prophetic insight on biblical truths that will open the understanding of readers, regardless of age, race, denomination, or spiritual maturity. In the 21st chapter of Matthew, the Kairos time represented the time in which fruit was ripe to be received by the reaper. Kairos is the ancient Greek word meaning the right or opportune moment.

In a day and age in which the divine identities of men, women, and families have been challenged by the doctrines of this age, the need for anointed teaching on relationships is critical and this book is being birthed in this Kairos time. The revelation of the Blueprint is coming forth in a time in which it will bless a multitude of generations.

Readers will enjoy the Blueprint's presentation on the roles and definitions of men and women that have been captured in the Bible. Lost identities have been recaptured in the pages of this book, and it will bring those who are lost back to the basic foundation of manhood and womanhood. As people understand the true intent of their identity, they will be able to have healthy relationships that have synergy that can give birth to a chosen generation. David's hallmark recipe for healthy relationships of *leave*, *love*, *give*, and *serve* provides a practical blueprint for establishing a healthy relationship and family unit.

Many marriages end because of selfishness and a lack of understanding by both husbands and wives. In addition to providing building blocks for relationships, David presents advice to single people who struggle with the sexual vices of being single and how to enjoy the biblical mandate of abstinent relationships.

David Burrus has been called to minister to this generation on the subject of relationships. He has a passion to bring simplicity and practicality to the deep and hidden mysteries that are locked within scripture. I have known David for nearly thirty years and he has always been a unique individual who was gifted in pioneering new paths and being fearless in pursuing the desires of his heart. He is a modern day leader who is in the midst of establishing the kingdom of God in the region that God has planted him in. The relevance of his ministry is found in reaching *Generation X* and the *Millennials*. *Generation X* and the *Millennials* are the generations of people who were born between the mid-1960s and the late-1990s. God has given David specific insight and wisdom that has the ability to capture the generations to which he has been called.

Table of Contents

CHAPTER ONE

Let Us Make Man

Why On Earth Am I Here?

There are very few things that are more dangerous to the world than a man who asks the question, "***Why on earth am I here?***" This question can lead a man down the path of wasted time and multiple regrets. When a man (or anyone for that matter) hasn't discovered who was created to be, he leaves himself open to become what his environment thinks he should be. A dear friend of mine, Dr. Lavian Coleman PhD., told me years ago, "Find a niche or a niche will find you."

God placed a distinctive assignment on every man's life, and many spend a lifetime trying to realize what that assignment (niche) is.

Oftentimes when you ask a man who he is, he will respond by telling you what he does. Many believe that in some way their resume and accomplishments validate their character and integrity, which could not be further from the truth. In fact, we are finding that success and accolades minus character and integrity are accidents waiting to happen. One of the premier intellectuals of our time, Dr. Myles Munroe, stated: "Where purpose is unknown, abuse is inevitable." When you haven't fully comprehended the purpose for why something exists, you have the proclivity to use it incorrectly, even to the point of abuse. When a man has not identified his purpose in life he will undoubtedly abuse his life and the time that he was given to fulfill his purpose. While a man may be experiencing what he and the society that he is a member of considers success, if he is not fulfilling his divine purpose in the earth, he is failing. The question then must be asked, "***Why on earth am I here?***"

Please make no mistake, God calls men to be doctors, sanitary workers, lawyers, pastors, activists, and philanthropists, just to name a few occupations. But there is a higher call on every man's life. Genesis 1:26 speaks directly to that higher call when it states, "And God said let us make man in our image, and after our likeness: and let them have dominion…" When we pay careful attention to the wording in this particular text, we get an even deeper revelation of who God desired for men to be.

The scripture indicates that we were made (not created) in His image. When something is created, it is fashioned without any blueprint or pattern. But when something is made, it is a duplicate of an original type or pattern. Its functionality is a direct reflection of its origin. God made mankind to enforce the same dominion and authority that He would enforce in the earth. God's original intent for man and mankind was to be His mouth, hands and feet in the earth. We are His direct representatives in the earth. That's important to note, because it is a reminder that our existence was not by happenstance. When God formed and fashioned us, He did so with a clear understanding of our intended function and purpose in the earth.

I could spend the rest of the book zeroing in on the relationship between a man and his God, but that is not the crux of my assignment as it relates to The Blueprint. I would like to spend the next few minutes highlighting what I think it is that a man was purposed and destined to do for his community, and specifically for his family. That which I am about to outline is what I refer to as the *Five Pillars of the Godly Man*. I believe that every man was called to operate in these five areas of his life.

Five Pillars of the Godly Man

The Priest

Whether he is a single man or a married man, he has been called of God to be the personal priest of his home. His responsibility as the priest is to keep himself morally clean so that he might be readily available to ***enter into the presence of the Lord on behalf of the people.*** The priest intercedes to God on behalf of the people. If he is a single man, he is called to intercede for those in his community, in his family, in his church and those closely connected to him. If he is a married man, he is responsible to intercede for those around him, but more importantly, for those in his household.

It is important for a single man to know that although he may not be married at the time, it is never too early to begin covering his future family in prayer. He can and should spend time praying for his children, and his children's children. He should spend time breaking the yoke of generations past, and pronouncing blessings over the lives of his future offspring. On the same note, the married man has a responsibility to take his family to the Lord in prayer on a consistent basis. This is important because there will undoubtedly come a time in his walk when he is not in the mood to pray for himself, and he will certainly encounter times when he is not in the mood to pray for others. He must remember that he is the watcher on the wall for his family, and if they are going to be safe spiritually and physically, he cannot afford to relinquish his post on the wall of intercession. This is the assignment of the priest of the home.

The Prophet

We understand that the priest of the home has the assignment of going to God on behalf of the people, but the prophet on the other hand has the responsibility of **speaking to the people on behalf of God**. This assignment works hand in hand with that of the priest. It gives a clear indication though, that the man of God can't be so given to speaking to God that he doesn't have an ear to hear from God. The prophet must be positioned to hear clearly from his Heavenly Father, and have the wisdom and ability to convey that which he has heard to the people who he has been given the charge to cover (mainly his household). Much like Noah, there are specific instructions that the Lord will give to the household only through his men. This is certainly not to belittle or minimize the woman's ability and/or anointing, but because God has created the man to lead his household, He often sends directives to the man first through his time of prayer and meditation.

For a single man to hear from God concerning his family, he must first have the capacity to hear from God concerning himself. Among other reasons, God often uses this time of singleness and solitude to develop his capacity to hear His voice and respond accordingly. When you consider the life of Adam as a single man (before Eve's arrival), his primary objective was to hear from God and respond to the voice of God. His livelihood literally depended on his ability to hear and follow the instructions of his Creator. As single men, I charge you to practice the presence of God. Your family's livelihood will ultimately depend on your ability to hear and implement that which you have heard from your Father in Heaven.

I must warn you that as the prophet of your home, your decisions will often come under great scrutiny. There will undoubtedly come a time when the response of *the people* will cause you to second-guess whether or not you have heard from the Lord. It's in those moments that you have to have an assurance that your ear is in-tune with the voice of the Lord, and that your heart is pure enough to discern when He's speaking and when He is not. God is honored when He can use the voice of the man to empower, encourage, instruct, discipline, comfort, console, direct, and change atmospheres. One of the most powerful weapons that a household could ever possess doesn't come with bullets or a holster, but it is a man who has spent time with the Lord, and one who will stand flat-footed to boldly declare what the Lord is saying.

The Protector

One of the man's key functions within the household is protector. His presence in the home should bring a certain measure of peace, security and soundness of mind to his family, and especially to his wife. There are two levels of protection for which a man must be willing to stand on the wall.

The man is called to protect his household physically. This means he is to ensure that whether he is home or away from the home, security measures and systems are in place, which will allow his family to rest in knowing that they are free from harm. As harsh as my next statement will sound, it is something that must be stated – A man is also responsible for protecting his family from himself. When a household feels more secure when that man is away from the home, there is a major breakdown in the very fiber of that household.

Not only is the man responsible for protecting his household physically, but also spiritually. It is his responsibility to stand on the wall of spiritual warfare for his family. It is not the wife's responsibility to be the spiritual leader of the family, but that is the man's responsibility. Whether he realizes it or not, the man is the pastor of his home. He shepherds his household to a safe and secure place as he is moving the vision forward.

The Provider

I won't waste much time belaboring a very simple concept. Men are definitely called to provide for their household. This becomes an interesting dichotomy because we are living in a day and age when women have the potential to make just as much, if not more than men do. What's even more interesting is that in many cases, single women come into the relationship having already established a very secure life for themselves. Many have forfeited a relationship to remain single, living up to the "***What can a man do for me?***" mentality.   It is certainly not to say that women can't do for themselves, but it is to say that they shouldn't have to if there is a man who is willing to lighten her load by supporting her in any way that he can.

There are obviously several valid scenarios why a man might not have the ability to provide for his family, but there is no excuse for a man who doesn't desire to provide. In Ephesians 5:25, husbands were given instruction to ***"love your wives as Christ loved the church, and gave His life for her."***   In other words, we have a spiritually lawful responsibility to ensure that they have what they need. I used to wonder why women get so anxious under financial hardships, while their husbands don't break a sweat and view it as ***not a big deal***. But we must consider the state that Eve was in when she met Adam. When Eve was presented to Adam in Genesis, everything had already been provided for her.   She lacked absolutely nothing. God had given Adam the assignment to work the Garden, yet Eve's assignment was to enjoy the Garden. Adam was used to the sowing and reaping process, yet Eve was never given that assignment and she found it foreign to her. She went from God's hand to her husband's hand, and never experienced the hand of struggle.

Please be mindful of the Father's instructions to His sons concerning His daughters, and to the daughters concerning His sons. He instructs wives to submit to their husbands. He makes this a requirement because women were created to have equal power, dominion, and authority as men (Genesis 1:28). On the other hand, His instruction to the husband is that he loves his wife even to the point of giving his life for her, even as Christ did for His bride, the church. The ultimate expression of love is giving, and the ultimate gift is one's life. This is the essence of provision. If a man will provide his life as a sacrifice for his bride, there's nothing that he won't give to see that she is provided for. Men are undoubtedly called to provide.

The King

Men are called to be the King of their households (kingdom). In our western civilization, we don't have a very clear concept of how a king and his kingdom function. And while I can't spend much time focused on how a kingdom operates, I can tell you that the word king speaks to dominion and order. Those two words summarize the function of a king and his relationship to his kingdom.

Kings establish dominion. In other words, they establish and enforce the laws and the boundaries of that kingdom. They don't need to do it forcefully, because their rank and authority speaks for itself. If a man has to say "I'm the man of this house," he's probably not.

Kings establish order. When a king walks into a room, people stand to attention. They stand, acknowledging that someone of importance has entered the room. Kings bring order with them. When a man walks into his home, all things should come to order. The dog should stop barking, the children should behave, and his wife should feel safe, because the king has returned to the kingdom.

Men of Purpose

If you have been around Christian settings, and primarily church environments, you have probably heard by now and understand that Eve was purposed to be a ***helpmeet*** to Adam. In other words, her assignment was to assist Adam in fulfilling his assignment. Upon close inspection of Genesis, we find that Eve was not presented to Adam until Adam understood and began to comply with the assignment that God had clearly placed on his life. Eve was created, but she had not been presented until Adam was following after the instructions that the Lord had charged him to do. This is likely why women get so bored with a man who has very little going on in his life. She was created to "help". But if he has nothing to help with, it can cause her to become antsy in the relationship. If he isn't giving her anything to help with, she will help herself.

When the Lord desired to deliver unto Adam his helpmeet, He did something that I find most peculiar. He put Adam to sleep. Adam was so involved in his Kingdom assignment, and so enthralled by the work that was before him, that he had to have his purpose interrupted to bring the missing link to the purpose, his help. In other words, Eve came as an interruption, and sleep (the first anesthesia) was needed to tranquilize this mover and shaker long enough to give him what he needed to ultimately succeed. Eve could not come until Adam had rested long enough to receive her.

It is important for single men reading this to know that you must know, understand and be operating in your purpose in order for your future helpmeet to maximize her potential concerning you. If she has come to help you get **there**, yet you don't know where **there** is, how is she supposed to feel secure in you or in her place in the relationship? Does this mean that men have to have every component of their divine assignment worked out? Absolutely not. It does mean that you are aware that God has called you to greater, and that greater will come as you apply pressure to your purpose. Then, and only then, should a single man feel secure enough to attach a purpose driven woman to his life.

What I am going to say next may shock you, but if you research it you will find that it's quite true. Are you ready? Adam never asked for a wife. In fact, you never read where Adam even requested any type of companion. I'm inclined to believe that Adam was quite satisfied with his relationship with his Heavenly Father, and his assignment given to him by his Heavenly Father. It was the Lord's suggestion in Genesis 2:18 that ***man should not be alone***; it wasn't the man's idea. Marriage was God's idea. Please note that Adam was never lonely, but he was always alone. Again, Adam was quite satisfied being a man alone and operating in purpose. It is more important for man to know his purpose before he knows whom he is intending to marry. I would even say that a relationship in which the man lacks purpose is a relationship that is founded on unstable ground.

13

When Eve arrived on the scene we never read where she inquired of Adam concerning his purpose. Neither do we ever read where Adam had to stop what he was doing to catch her up to speed in regards to his purpose. Because she was called and assigned to assist him in it, and because when she showed up he was already operating in it, there needed to be no debriefing. When a man is functioning in the assignment by which he has been called, no one ever has to question what that assignment is. That's simply because it's not what he does but it's who he is. You may need to inquire concerning the details, but if you watch him long enough, his purpose will speak for itself. Likewise, it's a dangerous thing for a woman to know a man, and yet still have to inquire about who and what he is called to be or do.

Proverbs 18:22 states *"**Whoever finds a wife finds something good and has obtained favor from the Lord.**"* A man who finds his helpmeet steps into a new level of favor for his calling. When he receives his wife the Heavens open up on his behalf. Why such favor you might ask? There is now a new favor to fulfill the assignment that has been placed on his life that begins first with his family, and then with those in his community.

Think about this for a moment. Adam was so very content with being a single man operating in purpose that he never made mention of a companion. God his Father not only knew that he would need a companion, but he knew what Adam would need in a companion to be satisfied. God knows who you need to fulfill the purpose that He's placed inside of you. He also knows exactly whom He has anointed to minister to your spiritual, intellectual and emotional needs. When we begin to trust God more, and rely on our own thought processes less, we will begin seeing relationships that thrive from beginning to end.

Speaking of Being the Provider

When we look at the process whereby God presented Eve to Adam, we must pay careful attention to the order by which He chose to do it. Before God presented Eve to Adam, He gave Adam a source of perpetual provision. That source of perpetual provision is outlined for us in Genesis 2:10. It reads, *"And a river went out of Eden (the garden) to water the garden; and from thence it was parted and became four river heads."* Did you catch what happened there? Out of Adam's home was a resource that divided into four individual resources that were designed to feed the lifecycle of the garden. There were four rivers, or four sources of income, that were placed strategically so that Adam's home would never suffer lack.

Where there is water, there's vegetation; where there is vegetation, there are trees; where there are trees, there is fruit; where there is water and fruit, there are animals; where there are animals, there is meat, and flesh for shelter or clothing. Do you see where this is going? There were for streams that flowed, so that if one dried up, was blocked, or even interrupted, there were three other sources of life and income. As men of God, we have a responsibility to allow the resources that we have in our home to become sources of life for our home. Whether those resources come in talent or treasure, we must make certain that they are producing life and provision for our households. God has placed enough in us as men that we don't ever have to rely on one stream of income to provide for us. We can, must and will pull what God has given us to open up other avenues to bring us the wealth that God has promised us. Your job will never be able to afford the assignment that is on your life as a man called to the world.

We must be careful to remember that God is the source and we are the resource. He gives us the streams of income and requires us to be great stewards of them. When God gave Eve over to Adam's care, He placed the responsibility to always have provision readily available to her. That provision started at the streams. I can't stress it enough that there are enough gifts and talents inside of all of us to be wealthy and to never have to work another day in our lives. I encourage every man to discover and cultivate those hidden treasures. When you discover who you are and maximize what you do, you will discover the resources that will assure that you have what you need.

Adam didn't have to create the streams; he simply had to cultivate them. It is never our responsibility to provide for ourselves. It is, however, our responsibility to make certain that we are being the best stewards over what God has given to us to manage. Adam didn't have anything to do with the garden or the streams being there, but he had everything to do with them staying there. I can't stress it enough; God will give us several streams of income and life, yet we must be wise enough to work what we have been given.

CHAPTER TWO

Bone of My Bone

More Than a Want

When we look at Genesis 2:7 and we consider the process by which God chose to bring Adam into the earth, there is something very interesting that is worth pointing out from that portion of scripture. It says, *"**And the Lord God formed man of the dust of the ground**."* Please note that the word ***formed*** when translated from Hebrew means ***distressed.*** We understand that the word ***distressed*** means ***in need of immediate help.*** From the moment that Adam was formed, there was a requirement placed in his DNA for a helpmeet. He didn't necessarily want a woman as much as he needed one.

If I could be candid for a moment, I speak from personal experience on this key point. I tell my wife all of the time that I love her dearly. But what I share with her even more is the fact that I really need her in my life. She brings to me a level of security that no other person brings. This security is not one of physical safety (although I do tend to sleep better when she is around), but of an emotional safety. Just to know that there is a person divinely appointed to tend to my needs emotionally bring me great peace and solitude. She consoles me when I am feeling low, and comforts me when I am felling a bit insecure. She celebrates me when I am doing well, and corrects me, in love, when I am on the wrong track. She was designed by God to be my helper or helpmeet, and these are all small yet important functions of a helpmeet.

A few months ago, a very dear friend of ours shared something with my wife and I that literally rocked us. It changed the dynamic of my wife's role in our marriage. She told my wife that she is to become my "personal prophet". What she was essentially saying is that Tanisha, my wife, should have a word for me from the Lord at any given moment. This is important because it challenges Tanisha, and any other wife for that matter, to stay in the face of the Lord for a word for her husband. Even as I have mentioned in chapter one that the husband is the prophet of his home, the wife is the personal prophet of her husband. Many would disagree with this fact, stating that the woman has no right giving the man instruction/direction from the Lord. But, my question is if he can't trust her to see and hear God for him, whom else can he trust to do so?

Just as Adam was formed in need of immediate help, so too is every man who is walking the face of the earth. God placed a natural system of nurturing in place from childbirth. The woman carries the man-child in her for 9 months. For those nine months he draws nutrients from her blood stream. He becomes familiar with her touch, the rhythm of her heart beat, and even her comforting voice. For nine months, his survival is predicated on how well she protects him as he matures enough to fend for himself. Even when he is born, he gains nutrients from sucking milk from her full breasts. As the man-child matures, he relies on the women in his environment to coach and train him in the area of his emotions. Men often perform better when the women that they love (mother, daughter, wife, girlfriend, friend, etc.) are watching in support. Why is that? It's because from a child even until adulthood, men draw strength from the presence of women. I say it all of the time, if a woman ever wants to see her man move a mountain, she merely has to tell him that he can, and he undoubtedly will.

It's not that Eve was to help Adam with the manual work that was assigned him, but rather, to support him emotionally as he worked the purpose and destiny that was attached to his life. She was just as vital to his purpose as he was. There were certain things that Adam was to begin fulfilling prior to her arrival, but his ultimate purpose was to be fulfilled while they were together, a unit of one. That's certainly not to say that she completed him, because she didn't. God completed Adam, but she assisted Adam in completing his God given assignment in the earth. It is important for single women to know that you are more than just a woman; you are the key to unlock someone's full potential. If you ever want to see a woman agitated in a relationship, place her in a relationship with a man that has nothing going on. Her assignment is to help him do what he is called to do. But, what does she do when he is not doing anything of significance? That is an accident waiting to happen. A woman that was created to be a helpmeet, needs something to help with, or the relationship might just become helpless.

Incubator

Women have the unique ability to do what a man could never do, and that is the ability to *incubate*. Let's define the word *incubator* for a moment, in order that we might grasp the magnitude of such an awesome and miraculous assignment.

in.cu.ba.tor (noun): **1** *an apparatus for maintaining an infant, especially a premature infant, in an environment of controlled temperature, humidity, and oxygen concentration* **2** *a place or a situation that permits or encourages the formation and development, as of new ideas.* A woman's body has been designed, formed, and structured to serve as an incubator that holds, nurtures and develops cells to full grown infants.

There is a grave difference between a woman, a wife and a helpmeet. Any woman has the ability to birth a man's children, but only a God ordained wife has the ability to birth his vision. Even as an incubator creates a safe environment for a developing fetus, thought, or idea; so too does a wife's spirit create a safe environment for her and her husband's vision to reach the state of maturity even as it develops. She has the ability to nurture it through prayer to maturity, and nurse it to health from her bosom of intercession and supplication.

One of the greatest mistakes that a husband could make is to not share the vision that the Lord has given him with his wife. Often times we as men are afraid that the vision will frighten them, cause them to waver in their faith, and/ or cause them to look at us like we are strange for think- ing/believing for something so grand or minute. But the truth is, her spiritual womb is strong enough and delicate enough to handle the vision that God is placed in you. It is the husband's responsibility to impregnate his wife with spiritual vision, purpose, and destiny. When a man and a woman become one flesh, his vision becomes her vision, and her vision becomes his vision. Each individual plays an equal role in caring for the well being of the vision. Her role is to safely carry the vision to full term, and his role is to assure that she has the spiritual vitamins and climate that she needs, as the incubator, to assure that the vision is healthy through the entire pregnancy. Her assignment is not just to his vision, but it is also to her own vision as well. Contrary to popular belief, God called and assigned women to do great things in the Kingdom of Heaven and in the earth. And just as she is to guard her husband's vi- sion with her life, she is to also guard her own vision with her life.

I am most certain that there are single women who are reading this thinking, "But what if I am not married?" What do I do with my spiritual incubator if I don't have a husband's vision to carry? I think that it is important for every woman to know that you are loaded with purpose and destiny. There are so many things that the Lord wants to birth through you as a single woman of God, and it is incumbent of you to maximize the time that you have birthing your Father's vision first. Many single men and women make the mistake of rushing out of singleness into marriage, to meet a person's needs when they haven't satisfied the needs of their Father. Be your Heavenly Father's number one incubator. When He impregnates you with vision, carry it through and birth it when He requires you to birth it.

I can recall being a single man and doing something that most would find strange or even peculiar. Although I didn't know who she was, I would pray blessings over my future wife. But more importantly, I would pray blessings over her spiritual and natural womb. My prayer is that she would have the same capacity to carry and birth vision that she did to carry and birth children. That everything that flowed through her womb would be healthy, prosperous, and that it would not abort under pressure. I encourage my single men that are reading this to begin praying and pronouncing spiritual and natural blessings over your future spouse.

It's important that you cover your incubator in prayer before you meet them and after you are together, remembering that it's their womb that births your seed. Women are incubators, and they have been given the divine authority to birth; which is a simple way of saying that God performs miraculous works through the minds, bodies, and spirits of women.

Don't I Know You From Somewhere?

As my wife and I have grown together and matured together over the years, we've heard time and time again that we have begun to resemble each other. While it is that we don't necessarily see it and/or agree with what others see, we can fully understand why people might say that. In my research of marriage and relationships, and especially as I explore relationships from a biblical perspective, I have found something key that supports the "look alike" theory.

When we take a look at Genesis we read the words, "*Male and female created He them. And God blessed them and told them be fruitful, multiply, replenish, subdue, and have dominion.*" In His creative process, the Lord chose to empower him, her, and them. Adam was empowered to operate as God's man in the earth. Eve was empowered to operate as God's woman in the earth. The two of them were empowered to operate as God's union in the earth. They had separate functions for a common goal; to establish Kingdom authority in the earth. This purpose was spoken at the same exact time over both of their lives. Now let's fast forward to the point when we are introduced to Adam.

When we are introduced to Adam in the book of Genesis, we find him working in partnership with God the Creator, naming the animals. What's in interesting is that Adam was in complete union and communication with God, yet God referred to Adam as being alone. He was so very concerned about Adam's wellbeing that He said to Himself, *"It is not good for man to be alone."* It is then that we are introduced to Eve, the one that was created for Adam. We have to pay careful attention to the response of Adam as he meets his wife/companion for the first time. We read Adam's response in Genesis 2:23 where he said, *"This is now bone of my bones, and flesh of my flesh: she shall be called Woman, because she was taken out of Man."* How is it that Adam, who'd had no prior contact with another human being, could immediately recognize Eve as being his equal? How is it that he never viewed her as a stranger, but from the moment that he met her he viewed her as the one that completed him? It almost appeared that he'd known her his entire life, and that they were being reunited once again. The underlying question that holds such rich revelation is how can two complete strangers meet, and feel like they have known each other for their entire lives?

The answer is quite simple, yet quite complex. Genesis 1:27-28 says, "*So God created man in His own image, in the image of God created He him; male and female created He them. And God blessed them, God said unto them, be fruitful, and multiply, and replenish the earth, and subdue it…*" Chapter 2:7 follows up with the plan of God by saying, "*And the Lord God formed man of the dust of the ground…*" The answer to our million dollar question is found in these three verses. God made man first and then woman, but He created male and female at the same exact time. To create means to establish or develop something having no pattern, yet to make the means to recreate a model or pattern. Mankind was designed to perform the same role in the earth as the invisible God performs in Heaven, which is the creative process. But woman was designed to be a duplicate of man. You're probably wondering by now, what this has to do with the initial question of how two complete strangers can feel like mates from the moment that they meet.

We understand that Adam was formed first, and Eve was formed second. But, where was Eve in the time between the moment that Adam was formed and the moment that she was formed? She was inside of Adam, waiting to be presented. They were one flesh spiritually, even before they were one flesh naturally. As Adam spoke, she became familiar with his voice. As Adam's heart changed beats, she became familiar with what excited him and what calmed him. During Adam's communion with the Lord, she became acquainted with his style of prayer, praise and worship.

At the exact moment that they met in the flesh, he knew clearly who she was, and she undoubtedly knew who he was. They were looking at reflections of themselves. When Adam met Eve, he was essentially meeting himself for the first time. When Eve met Adam, she too was meeting herself for the very first time. This is why they never questioned neither did they doubt that they were the ones for each other. Adam quickly declared that she was the one that he'd been waiting for. When there is a divinely appointed union between a single man and a single woman, there will be no questions about it. The only promises that are guaranteed are those that are found in the will of the Lord. When we surrender our will to the Lord's, and allow Him to make the connections, He brings us into doubt-free situations.

The Revelation of the Rib

We are given front row seats to the process by which God chose to bring woman into being, and it is an interesting process to say the least. In Genesis 2:21 we read, ***"And the Lord God caused a deep sleep to fall upon Adam, and he slept: and He took one of his ribs, and closed up the flesh instead thereof."*** I am certain that there are people that have read this for the first time, and those that have read it for the one thousandth time, that have walked away with the same exact question every time. Why did the Lord choose to form and fashion woman out of a simple little rib out of the man's side? You might even be one of those that can't quite wrap your mind around the concept of a woman being formed out of a man's rib. Your answer is on the way.

My wife and I have held countless seminars, classes and

workshops on marriage and relationships to both the single audience and married audiences. We've touched on many topics and have even customized sessions for the specific needs of the audience that we are speaking with. I must admit that what we are about to discuss next is something that we seem to always include in these sessions, simply because it has become one of our favorite things to discuss. I am talking about the infamous **rib** that woman was formed from. There have been many myths about whether or not God used an actual rib, or if it is merely symbolic. There have been scientific debates as well as theological debates about the subject. There have been archeological debates and psychological discussions concerning the rib. Nothing interests me as much as the revelation that comes from the Holy Spirit about why He may have chosen the rib. What I will share with you over the next couple of pages is not designed to prove or disprove any of the above schools of thought. It is on the other hand presented that you might have a fresh and divine revelation of why God may have chosen the rib, as opposed to any seemingly more logical member of the human body to use to form the woman.

When we get an understanding of why God the Creator chose to use the rib to form the woman, we will undoubtedly have a deeper insight of the responsibility that the man has towards the woman, and the woman towards the man in the grand scheme of things concerning the marriage relationship. There are five key functions of the rib to the human body, so let's take a look to see how they speak to us in our current and future relationships.

Revelation #1: The rib is irreplaceable. You cannot grow another rib. In the relationship, there is not another thing that can replace the function of the woman. No drug can do it, no pornographic material can do it, and certainly no other man can do for the man what a woman can do for him. When God made woman for man, He was essentially saying that He was presenting a one of a kind to him. You must remember that Adam was surrounded by animals, yet there were none that could meet his physical, psychological, intellectual, emotional or spiritual needs. The Lord presented Adam with a one of a kind, irreplaceable gift that would meet his every need.

Revelation #2: The rib is directly connected to the spine. We understand that the spine is the support system of the body, and when the spine falters, the body will soon follow. It is critical to note that throughout a man's lifespan, he is most successful when there is a strong woman that is willing to support his vision. If a woman ever wants to see her man conquer a mountain, she merely has to tell him that he can and he will. From the time that he is a child relying on his mother to support him emotionally, until he is a grown man relying on the women in his life to continue to support him, most men are only as strong as the women that are willing to support them.

Revelation # 3: The rib is located at the side. This is important because the woman wasn't created to lead him from the front, or be subservient from behind, but she was created to walk side by side with him through life. Eve was Adam's life partner. God didn't just bless Adam, and just give Adam dominion, but they both received the blessing of the Lord. The woman was divinely appointed by God to partner with man in the dominion of the earth.

Revelation #4: The rib is located at the center of the body. She wasn't formed out of the skull to Lord over the man, and neither was she formed out of the feet to be trampled on by the man. She was fashioned from that which is at the center of the body which means she is in complete balance with the man.

Revelation #5: The rib is located under the arm. A woman should find safety and security in the presence of her man. The rib is located under the arm, which is symbolic of security, protection and covering. It was God's intent for the woman to have a sense of total comfort and security when her man is present. She should find financial security, emotional security and physical security in the presence of her man. It was never the will of God for the woman to be afraid or anxious when the man comes around. When that is the case we have fallen far from the plan of God for our relationships.

Revelation #6: The rib covers the heart. Men are warriors. We are hunter-gatherers. We spend the majority of our lives in the world competing and fighting to survive. We compete on our jobs and even amongst our friends. If we were to be completely honest, it often takes the sensitivity and nurturing heart of a woman to tame the wildness in our hearts. God created the woman to cover us in those vital areas of our lives, and to tend to our hearts. There are often places of vulnerability that we can explore with our women that we could never explore with our male friends. Every strong man needs a strong woman in his corner to cover his heart.

As you can see, it's quite obvious that God knew exactly what He was doing when He opted to use the rib. The bottom line is, men need women. Society would like us to believe that women are here merely to fulfill our sexual desires, but that is an absolute lie. It is only a shallow minded person that desires to limit a woman only to what she can perform while on her back. It is only when men appreciate and value what women bring into the relationship, that we can begin treating with the love and respect that is due them.

He That Finds a Wife

There are a myriad of reasons on why I enjoy the teaching aspect of what I do, but there are few things that I find more exciting than teaching singles about godly relationships. In my many years of teaching singles about relationships, I seem to somehow always end up answering what I call the fifty million dollar question. It's the question that everyone wants to know, many take the risk of asking, and very few are patient enough to wait on the answer for. The fifty million dollar question is, "***How will I know when I have found the one?***" This question, my friend, has the potential to single-handedly end the epidemic that we call divorce.

If I could be transparent for a moment, I can recall being a young man in ministry, and having a constant desire to be married. I desired to be married because I always longed to experience the love that I'd seen exhibited in the lives of so many other young Christian couples that I'd seen and admired from afar. I also understood that the sexual frustration that I was feeling as a healthy young man would finally be over. There were several other reasons why I thought that it was important that I find the woman that was designed to walk with me through life. While this is a noble desire, and few men are actually rushing out of singleness, I must admit that I didn't go about it the correct way. Because I didn't go about it the correct way, there were many emotional casualties along the way. So, what was I doing wrong?

I was doing what I find many eager single men and women like me doing. I was seeking the Lord for a companion, even going so far as to fast and pray, yet I would move on a relationship before receiving my instruction or my answer. Many might ask, what's wrong with being single and playing the field? We will cover the in-depth answer to that in chapter seven, but to answer that in short we must exam the instruction that has been afforded us in Proverbs

18:22. It reminds us that, "*He that finds a wife finds what is good, and receives the Lord's favor*." So, how exactly does that statement speak to the question at hand, "*How will I know when I have found the one?*" And even more importantly, how does one keep from making the mistake of choosing the wrong mate? Let's take a closer examination of Proverbs 18:22 to gain more insight.

When you *find* something you get it by searching or making an effort. It implies that something is hidden or tucked away, and in need of being discovered or uncovered. The question then must be asked, if God smiles on healthy Christian marriages, and He uses the institution of marriage to model His relationship with His church, why would he require the woman to be hidden? Please know that He never desired for her to be lost, but rather, that she be hidden. It has always been God's desire that his single daughters be tucked away and hidden safely in Him. We see this example throughout the Bible, with Eve being our first and primary example. There was never a point in her single life that she was outside of the presence of God. There was also never a time in Adam's single life that he was outside of the presence of God. They were both lost in Him.

Because Eve was hidden in Christ, the only way that Adam to get to her was to go through Christ. And, because Adam was hidden in Christ, the only way that Eve was able to recognize that he was the one was because it was her father, God, which led her down the aisle to her groom. Adam found his wife, and she was hidden in God. If Christian singles really desire to make the right choice when it comes to their relationships and future marriages, they must allow the Holy Spirit to navigate them and to lead them to each other. It's when we become our own navigation systems that we place ourselves in grave danger of making terrible choices that we may regret for the rest of our lives.

It's also important to mention that Proverbs 18:22 never makes mention of the man finding a girlfriend. It suggests that he was in search of a wife. If we refer to the relationship of Adam and Eve, we discover that Adam never dated Eve. When he met her, he met his wife. When she met him, she met her husband. They were literally made for each other, and they complimented each other. I think that it is important that I point out that if a godly man is in search of his godly mate, he should never make the mistake of seeking a girlfriend that would one day make a good wife. He needs to be in search of a wife that would also make a great girlfriend. Please don't misunderstand what I am saying. I am in no way implying that he should be seeking out another man's wife to make her his wife. That would be completely contrary to the will of God. What I am saying is that it is important that a man looks beyond his current need when considering whom his wife will be. It's also safe to say that not every woman that is hidden in Christ is being hidden for him. Just because she would make a good godly wife, doesn't necessarily mean that she would make a good godly wife for him. This is why it is so very critical that both the man and the woman allow God to be the center of everything that they do as individuals, so that He can navigate them into everything that they will do as a unit.

Speak Over Me

One afternoon I was researching the book of Genesis, as I often do, for nuggets that speak to marriage and relationships, when something very interesting leaped out at me. It was one of those nuggets that could be so very easily overlooked, yet it is the answer to so many singles questions. I must admit that when I discovered it, it revolutionized the way that I teach single Christians in the area of relationships. When we look at Genesis chapter two, we are afforded a backstage pass into the formation of the marriage institution. We are literally witnessing the very first wedding. We have the Father that presents His daughter to her husband, and literally gives her away. In Him giving her away, he is essentially saying that He has found a man of character and integrity that He is certain will cover and protect her all of her days. This is what every father desires for his daughter. What was most shocking to me is Adam's reaction as he took his wife's hand in marriage.

In Genesis 2:23, Adam responds by saying, "*This is now bone of my bones, and flesh of my flesh.*" Adam immediately recognized who she was, and what she meant to him. He immediately identified with the role that she played in his destiny. He spoke with all certainty as if to say that that the one that I have been waiting for has finally arrived, although we never heard Adam request a wife. Adam recognized his bride by the God that was standing next to her holding her hand. When a man and a woman live God centered lives, there will never be a question or doubt as to whether or not this is the one that God is sending, because they will be lead of God and they will be standing next to Him when their spouse arrives.

When we dig a little deeper we discover an even weightier nugget, and an even clearer indicator that they were meant for each other. If you are single and reading this I want you to pay very close attention to what Adam did next. After declaring that she was "***bone of his bones, and flesh of his flesh,***" he said something that literally sealed the deal. He announces that, ***"She shall be called Woman, because she was taken out of man."*** In this moment, what we don't see happen is more important than what we do see happen. Notice that prior to and even at this point, we never hear where Adam touches his wife. What we did hear was that he used his words to touch her heart. Adam openly and publicly declared who she was to the world, even before he laid one finger on her. What's even more interesting is that by calling her Woman (womb-man), he spoke purpose and destiny over her life.

I want to speak to all of the single ladies that are reading this book right now. If you are wondering if he is the one, one of the many indicators is if he does what Adam did, which is to speak purpose over you. If he is more eager to reach you with his hands than he is to help you reach your destiny with his mouth, he may very well not be the one. You must remember that the man that God has for you, is a man that is after His heart. He's a man that spends time in His presence, and knows the voice of God. The man that God has for you is carrying your future and destiny in his heart, and is looking for his rib so that he can release it out of his mouth into your spirit. When you meet him, you will know him by what he does and does not do. Ladies, I encourage you to seek the Lord, not just for the man that has the physical attributes that you desire, and the financial stability that you need, but most importantly, the man that has your destiny in his mouth.

To my single brothers, I have some instruction for you as well. I encourage you to ask God to begin showing you your Eve's purpose and destiny. I charge you to seek God for an identifying Word that will instantly confirm that she is the one when you meet her. After reading this book, and applying the principles, you will know exactly who she is when you meet her. We all know that we men are often easily motivated by our sense of sight, and because we know this we can't afford to base any of our future relational decisions on what we see, because we know that looks can often be deceiving. When we look at examples of great men that followed after God, we are reminded of men like Moses, Noah and Abraham. The thing that all of these men had in common with each other is that they were all successful when they moved according to the Word of the Lord that was engrafted into their hearts. When a single man has gotten a God Word about his future spouse, and he begins to allow the Spirit of that Word to navigate Him, it is impossible for him to lose at anything and especially as it relates to his future relationship and marriage.

CHAPTER THREE
Single and Satisfied

The Rush

I am always astonished and pleasantly surprised when I come across a single man or woman that is perfectly content with being single. It amazes me, because I am fully aware of the fact that they are in the minority. The majority of singles that I meet are eager to lay their single pass down, and pick up the marriage license for a change. This is in part because I am dealing primarily with single Christians between the ages of 25-45 years old. Many of which are actually trying their very best to keep themselves sexually pure, and emotionally baggage-free. The major problem that I have discovered with dealing with singles, and especially in this age bracket, is that they fear that time is not on their side. The pressure of starting a family and becoming settled into the family structure can often eat away at them. The feeling of having accomplished everything that they have desired to accomplish except the spouse, the 2.5 kids and the white picket fence has a way of eating away at them. There is often this unspoken rush to the finish line of singleness, which often cause many singles to stumble across the line instead of finishing strong.

Many unhealthy marriages and toxic family structures have been formed out of what I call **the rush**. I have witnessed so many children born out of wedlock, and so many marriages end in divorce because they were byproducts of the rush. I have done premarital counseling for couples, and have openly informed some of them that I didn't think that they were good candidates for marriage at the time. Some responded by letting me know that they too were aware of the fact that that they weren't actually ready for marriage, but because of the fear and the pressure of spending a lifetime being single, they decided to take a chance at the roulette table of marriage. If we were to be completely honest, there have been countless suicides and attempted suicides, all because of the pressure of the rush. There are mental facilities and psychiatric wards that are full of people who caved in under the pressures of the rush. So what's up with the rush?

When you research the definition of the word **rush**, there are a couple of key words that stand out, and speak to the detriment of why one should hesitate to rush into any relationship or marriage. The word rush also embodies such words as *violently, excessively, rashly,* and also *recklessly.* I doubt that anyone would desire for these words to be a characterization of how they view relationships, yet many have rushed into and out of relationships like they were five o'clock traffic. And much like these four defining words, they have found their relationships to be among other things violent, excessive, rash and even reckless. It's interesting to note that many of the divorces that are the result of rushing into relationships have the proclivity to end up violent, excessive, rash and reckless.

When you get to the root cause of the rush, it can be summed up in two very simple words, *outside interference*. God has always had plans for every stage of our lives. That plan covers our first breath, our last breath, and everything in between. He started in Genesis by breathing into the nostrils of mankind, and He has continued to breathe in and on us throughout the ages. His breath in our body is not only a miracle, but it serves as a symbol of His ability to not only work around us but in us as well. It's safe to say that if He's God enough to create us, shape us, and breathe life into us, than He's God enough to sustain us.

That sustenance also includes but is not limited to our relationships. Anytime we allow another person, place, thing, or idea to be the lord over our decisions, we are yielding the results and the upkeep to that thing or entity that we have allowed to be the lord. When we allow romantic movies and television shows, magazine articles and love songs, or even conversations with others to drive us into a panic and force us to rush into wrong relationships, we now surrender the relationship to the lordship of those ***outside interferences*** to sustain it.

We must remember in all situations that God never changes, but we do. His plan for our lives never wavers, yet we tend to waver. His idea of who we desires for us to be with doesn't vacillate, yet our ideas do. There comes a point in time where you must make the decision of whether or not you are going to allow Him to be Lord of all, or Lord of nothing. If in fact He is Lord of all, than you must remember that He is also the Lord of time. He knows exactly what He has for you, and exactly when He desires for you to have it. The rush doesn't cause God to move any faster, yet it can cause you to receive slower simply because you have caused yourself to be dislocated from your place of purpose. Don't allow the rush to be the murderer of your destiny and purpose. Rest and relax in the perfect timing of God, and allow Him to be the Lord of love that releases in His perfect timing.

Alone, But Not Lonely

When a person is single, they have to decide within themselves whether they are going to find contentment in being alone, or suffer the torment of walking through life lonely. Perhaps you had no clue that there was a distinct difference in being alone and lonely. Let's take a moment to investigate these two words, and to discover the clear differences between the two. Many have suffered because they couldn't make the mental transition from being lonely to simply being alone. When we take a look back at Genesis 2:18, we hear the Lord informing us that from His point of view ***it is not for man to be alone.*** He never makes mention of man feeling lonely, but He does inform us that man was indeed alone. So, what is the difference between the two seemingly similar words?

The Webster's New World Dictionary defines ***alone*** as "***apart from anything or anyone else.***" It also means, "***without involving any other person.***" The word ***lonely*** on the other hand means "***unhappy at being alone; longing*** *for friends, company, etc.*" As we can clearly see there is a distinct difference between the two words. Imagine how cruel of God that He would create a being only to have him spend his time suffering as a lonely being. The truth is it was never God's desire for his creation to have feelings of loneliness. It wasn't His desire for his sons and daughters to stumble through life desiring companionship. Alone is a state of being, yet loneliness is a matter of the heart. Until a person learns to tame their lonely heart and find contentment in being alone, they will live a life of torment and complete and utter discomfort. I would even say that a person that needs companionship to live isn't really living at all.

When God created, shaped and formed Adam, they were instantly meshed together. Where you felt God is where you saw Adam. And where you saw Adam is where you felt the presence of God. God created the Garden of Eden because he desired a place where His presence could literally touch the earth. From the moment that Adam was conceived, the only intellectual companion that He had was the God that created him. He was so dependent on God that it took the mouth of God to deliver unto Adam his very first breath. He was shaped and molded by God, and he walked in the cool of the day with God. God was at the center of his life and his heart. This, is why as a single man, Adam never requested companionship, because he had the ultimate companion in God. What's interesting is that His companion was a Spirit, which is why the Spirit [God] classified him as being alone, although Adam had never experienced an alone day in his life.

Can you imagine what God was thinking as he is preparing to present this woman to this man? I can only imagine that God had weighed the magnitude of this relationship that was about to take place between this man and this woman. For so long God was the center and target of Adam's love. But, God loved Adam so very much that he decided to present a gift that could potentially cause Adam's heart to withdraw from loving Him, and to direct the thrust of his affection towards loving this new gift that He received called Woman. God's love for Adam, and His desire to see Adam experience ultimate fulfillment was what caused Him to present Eve to Adam. But through all of this, Adam was quite satisfied with his relationship with His Creator and the Lover of his soul.

Consider the fact that when God was going to perform

surgery on Adam, to extract his bride from his body and spirit, he put Adam to sleep. He understood that Adam had to be stopped so that he might be presented with love. Man was so busy satisfying his Creator that he needed to be anesthetized to pull out of him his next level. My question for my single brothers and sisters that are reading this book is, are you satisfied with being alone, just you and God? Or are you in a rush to connect to the person that has the potential to distract you from your relationship with God? Are you so enthralled with your Creator that your life needs to be placed on hold so that He can bless you, or are you in such a hurry to get to the blessing that you have placed your relationship with your God on hold? Are you okay with being alone, or are you sick of being lonely?

Both Adam and Eve were quite content in their singleness. It was God that desired that they meet, and not themselves. It was God that arranged their meeting; they didn't make it happen. It was God that selected them for each other; they had absolutely nothing to do with it. They were busy being alone and loving it. My prayer for those of you that are single and reading this book is that you would find contentment in being alone with God. I pray that no outside forces or pressures would cause you to rush out of His presence to get into someone else's presence. Adam and Eve were able to meet because they were willing not to meet.

Incomplete Assignments

I was praying and driving down the street one afternoon when the Lord began reminding me of assignments that He'd given me that I had not completed. He was also showing me how my incomplete assignments were hindering me from graduating to the next level. In other words, He couldn't bless me with what I was asking Him for because I hadn't been a good steward over what He'd already given me. Doesn't that sound just like a Father? I take great consolation in knowing that I am not the only one who has experienced setbacks as a result of disobedience. This has been happening since the beginning of mankind.

Most Christians clearly understand that marriage is a ministry, but very few have an understanding that singleness is a ministry as well. Paul's letter to the church at Corinth in 1 Corinthians 7:32-33 puts it this way: "***But I would have you without carefulness. He that is unmarried cares for the things of the Lord, how he may please the Lord.***

But he that is married cares for the things that are of the world, how he may please his wife." Paul made a clear distinction between the affairs of the single person and the affairs of one that is married. He laid out for us the truth of the assignment of those that are single. It is through these passages of scripture that we are made aware that not only do married couples have great assignments to each other, but that single people also have a great assignment, and that is to fulfill the work of the Lord while they are single.

We all know singles that struggle with the loneliness issue, some of which are reading this book right now. You must be willing to answer one of the most imperative questions that you can answer as a single person, and that question is, am I finished being single? Sure, you probably desire to be finished, but has God said that you were finished? Have you done everything that He has required of you to do as a single person? Have you fulfilled every requirement and prerequisite that He's given you as a single person? Just like school, it is a grave disservice to you for your instructor to pass you on to the next level when you have not fully completed or passed the tests and assignments for your current level. The same exact thing can be applied to your singleness.

I can't tell you what your assignment is; only God can do that. I can't tell you what your requirements are; only He can do that. What I can assure you of is that there is a great work for you to do while you are single, and have fewer cares to distract you from the assignment. Believe me when I tell you that if you would allow yourself to fall deeper in love with God, and chase hard after the assignment that He has for you while you are single, you would find the greatest fulfillment that you've ever experienced in your life.

Let's reflect on what those assignments may be. What is it that you may have started and did not finish? This could be your assignment. What is it that God instructed you to start that you never got to? This too could be your assignment. What is that thing that you know that you are great at and that you feel in some way or another called to do, that you haven't started doing yet? That too may be what you are required to complete while you are single. Have you considered the reality of Jesus' very own singleness? I believe one of the things that made Jesus' ministry so very powerful was that He was a single man. He was free to travel. He was free to leave early and stay out late. He was financially free to contribute to the work of the Kingdom. Jesus understood that there was plenty of work that needed to be done for the kingdom, and He did it. We never once hear Jesus complain about being single, alone or lonely.

In no way am I attempting to compare you to Jesus, or vice versa. On the contrary, what I am doing is telling you that Jesus' life serves as the ultimate example of what a strong Christian lifestyle can look like. We understand that He was tempted by everything that we are tempted by, yet He endured. I want to encourage you today by letting you know that you are on assignment, and you will succeed. There's a graduation to another level at the end of this assignment. Be thorough, and finish strong.

Time is on Your Side

Have you ever had the feeling that you were running out of time in life? Perhaps you have been in a career for so long, and you feel like it's time to make a career change. You may even feel a desire to go back and complete the educational goals that you'd set for yourself years ago. Maybe there was a business that you always dreamed of starting, but never had the courage or the resources to get the dream off of the ground. There are people that are reading this book that have battled with the idea of being single, and the uncertainty of whether they will spend the rest of their lives having never experienced marriage. The unfortunate thing is that for many, the nagging feeling of them running out of time has caused them to make hasty and rash decisions that they will regret for the rest of their lives.

I say that it is unfortunate because the reality is that it is merely a deception and a lie. Who in the world has the authority and the power to tell you when you are too old or too far gone to fulfill what is predestined for you to fulfill in your lifetime anyway? Who has the power to tell you when you should stop allowing your heart to desire and seek after what you have been told is yours? There isn't a person in the world that is sovereign enough to tell you what is and is not your destiny. The only person that has that power and sovereignty is God. The real question is, why do we allow every person, place, thing or idea to have more influence over our thought processes than we do the one true and living God?

The thing that we often forget when it comes to our purpose and destiny is that it was God that authored our destiny. It was He that spoke our lives into existence and called our purpose into being. He knows that end from the beginning. The wonderful thing about God the Creator is that He doesn't wait until you have a need to fulfill it. His divine providence is already in place. Your need has already been fulfilled in the supernatural realm, and you are not running out of time. On the contrary, you are actually on schedule to meet your destiny. Every step that you take and every move that you make is a step that you are making closer to your destiny. Wherever you are going, that's where you will end up.

Have you considered the fact that we serve an eternal God that has no boundaries? He isn't bound by space, resources, and He's definitely not bound by time. God is the author of time, and has never been bound by it. He controls it, and He controls what happens in it. When it comes to the divine plan of God, nothing happens too late or too early, but it happens right on time. We find ourselves in trouble when we attempt to force things to happen outside of the timing of God. When we do this, it's almost as if we are saying that we more intelligent than God, and that we know what's best for our own lives. We forget that He is the author and finisher of mankind and our faith.

There is a quick fix to the anxiety that comes as a result of us feeling like we are running out of time. That quick fix is to change your mind about your life and your future. The way that you change your mind about your life and future is by being transformed in your thinking. Philippians 2:5 reminds us to **"Let this mind be in you, which was always in Christ Jesus."** To find yourself satisfied in the will of God, wherever it has you, you have to find yourself thinking with the mind [Spirit] of God. There has to be an exchange from your thought process to his thought process. If ever you want to adopt the philosophy or thought process of another person, you must indoctrinate yourself in their words. If we are going to exchange our thoughts for Christ's thoughts, we must find ourselves consumed by His Word.

I encourage you to get out of your own way by getting out of your own time. Step into the divine timing of God, and train yourself to find complete fulfillment is seeking His will, and not your will, to be done in your life. I charge you to maximize the time and potential that you have as a single person. Make sure that you have done all of the things that He has required of you to do in this season. I would encourage you to take an inventory of the things that you desire to do while you are single and free to do them. Here are some questions that I often ask singles that I want to ask you today. Have you done all of the traveling that you would have liked to do? Have you met all of the people that you would have liked to have met? Have you experienced all of the adventures that you would have liked to experience as a single person? Remember that you are only single once. Maximize this time that you have alone with the Lord, because once you are married, you will never be single again.

CHAPTER FOUR

You First, Then Me

Why Did I Get Married?

There was a sequel of movies that were released by Tyler Perry entitled *Why Did I Get Married?* The movie follows the lives of four successful couples that all find themselves at a fork in the road of their relationships, and they have to finally confront and address the question, "Why did we get married?" While that is a story that appears on the big screen, and we are afforded the luxury of fast forwarding the scenes that we don't like and rewind the scenes that we do like, the unfortunate thing is that many of our marriages are mirror images of the ones in the movie. The frightening thing is that we don't have the luxury of rewinding, fast forwarding or pressing stop. We are living the reality, and there seems to be very little that we can do about it. What do you when you were once living the dream, and the dream has transitioned into a nightmare?

I have discovered that there are far too many couples that

can't answer the question, "Why did we get married?" There are many couples that are actually ashamed to answer the question because they understand that they don't have a solid enough reason as to why they chose to get married. There are those couples that started out getting married for the right reason, yet they ended up staying married for the wrong reasons. And of course there are those couples that knew exactly why they were getting married, and have succeeded at marriage because they were able to stick to the code of marriage.

I remember my childhood, and once finding an abandoned set of golf clubs. Of course because I had not been introduced to golf at that early age, I had no idea of the significance or value of the golf clubs that I found. Because I was like most every other kid at that age, I had a very creative imagination. Those golf clubs became swords and walking canes. They were guns and spears. Anything that you can image that a golf club could be used for in t he hands of a kid, that's what they were used for. The only problem is, someone had made an investment in them, and they weren't being used according to purpose. They were being used, and in essence they were being abused, because they were not being used for their intended purpose. Did you know that many of us are in emotionally and physically abusive relationships and marriages because we have gotten away from why God made the investment in the first place? If we are not careful we will use our marriages as tools to leverage our egos, rather than to exemplify Christ.

It's unfortunate but a true that many of us have gotten married for what we can get out of the deal. Some of us have gotten married for the sexual gratifications that are afforded us in the marriage. Others have done it because of the financial stability that may come as a result of marriage. There are even those that have gotten married for the sole purpose of having children. Let me first say that none of these are wrong, and the Bible substantiates all of them. There are several scriptures that support all three of these theories, and even more. To say that someone is wrong for getting married because of these reasons is not accurate. I will say, on the other hand, that to require these to be the foundation and substratum of why you got married is like building a straw house in a sand storm. It's an accident waiting to happen. None of these are strong enough to support a marriage solely, simply because every one of those is conditional. They are only as strong as their ability to be supported themselves.

So why did you get married? Single people, why do you want to get married? In this chapter we will discover why God intended for us to get married. It will serve as a guide for singles so that as they approach marriage, they have a spiritually founded gauge by which they can weigh their reasoning. For those of us that are already married, this chapter will do one of two things. It will either confirm why you are where you are, and why you are succeeding in the marriage the way that you are. Or, it will serve as a barometer by which you can make corrections in your marriage. This chapter is not designed to be an indictment, but a roadmap towards a successful marriage.

If you don't apply any other chapter in this book to your life, I encourage you to apply this chapter. Appling the principles of this chapter will open you up to a world of blessings, simply because it will allow the Holy Spirit to navigate freely through all of your affairs, and especially your relationship with the ones that you love. By the end of this chapter, you will be able to answer without any hesitation, "Why did I get married?" And if you are single you will be able to stand firm as you answer the question why do I want to get married? Get ready to be blessed.

The Recipe of a Healthy Relationship

Every holiday season my cousin makes her world famous sweet potato pie for the family dinners. And every year I act like I have lost my natural mind when I sit down to eat her sweet potato pie. One slice turns into two, and two slices somehow ends up being four, until there are no more slices to count or compare. I finally wizened up last year and asked her to make me my very own sweet potato pie. I need to interject that she is a business owner, and very active in the community, so her time is very limited. That being said, I put my request in for a sweet potato pie, and she agreed. After a couple of weeks of calling and reminding her, I realized that she was a little too busy to make them, so I asked her for the recipe. The unfortunate thing is that she got the recipe by watching her mother, so the recipe is not written down anywhere which would make it impossible to recreate what she makes.

I remembered that I have a Patti Labelle cookbook in the kitchen, and from what I understand, Patti knows her way around a kitchen. I decided to make a Patti Labelle sweet potato pie, and much to my surprise it turned out great. In fact I have made several since that first one, and they get better every time that I make them. But what was it that caused me to succeed? It wasn't that I had a taste for it, and neither was it that I had a burning passion to make one. The thing that caused me to win in that situation was that I had a resource that I could refer to that was consistent, never changing, and would always yield the same results as long as I followed the recipe. There is nothing in the world that guarantees greater success than having a manual, guide or a recipe that you can follow to victory.

There have been millions of books that have been written on relationships, and the majority of them are packed with rich and helpful information. Some of them take a more philosophical stance while others take a more psychological point of view. But whatever their point of view, one thing is certain, there are no shortage of books that deal with relationships. These are all great sources, but there is only one source. There is only one tried and true recipe that will yield lasting results time and time again. That recipe book is the Word of God. He's the author of relationships and has the final say when it comes to them. So, why spend time attempting to create something lasting from a word of mouth recipe, when we have direct access to the main source? Let's take a closer look at the recipe and ingredients for a winning marriage and relationship.

Leave. Love. Give. Serve.

One of the very first scriptures that many of us were introduced to was John 3:16 which states, "***For God so loved the world, that He gave His only begotten Son, that whosoever believes in Him would not perish but have everlasting life.***" We have seen it on bumper stickers, on coffee cups and even in the end zone at football games. I think that we have taken this scripture for granted without fully understanding the magnitude of it. I believe that if we would grasp and apply this scripture to our lives, our relationships would begin to look like what God intended for them to look like. I would go so far as to say that if we would apply this one simple scripture to our marriages, that there would be less divorce, abuse and abandonment. John 3:16 has become almost an elementary passage that we teach our children in order to fulfill our duties as good parents, but it is much more than that. Let's take a closer look to discover how it is actually the antidote for our relational problems.

There are four key ingredients that can be located in John 3:16 that lend themselves to healthy and fulfilling relationships. Those four ingredients are ***leave, love, give, serve.*** I assure you that if you apply these ingredients to any of your relationships, you will come with a winning outcome. Whether we are talking about your relationships with your co-workers, children, spouse, or even loved ones, the application of these four simple ingredients will change the outcome of every relationship that you will ever be involved in.

Like any recipe, it is not only important that the ingredients are applied, but that they are applied correctly. Many that are reading this book can honestly say that they have attempted to apply these to their lives and relationships, and this may very well be true. But, the objective of this chapter is to make sure that these four ingredients are applied to the love recipe accurately and with a heart that patterns God. It's possible to attempt to leave, love, give, and serve out of impure motives and this will only lead to destruction and heartache. We will take a close look at all four of these ingredients individually, in an attempt to gain a deeper insight on how they should be applied to your relationships.

Leave

When we read John 3:16, we are made aware of the deep and undying love of God for his creation. But, what is just as important to understand is the willingness of God to sacrifice His comfort in exchange for ours. Before God came to earth to die on the cross for our sins, he was in Heaven with His Father. He chose to put on flesh, and to leave all of the glory that is Heaven, to come to a sin-sick world to take on our sicknesses. He came to take on the weight of sin, that we might have an eternal life free of the penalties of sin. But why would He do that? How many people do you know that are willing to leave a place of comfort and security, and step into a place of discomfort and instability? Would you be willing to do that? Do you think that your spouse would be willing to do that? Do you think that the lady at the checkout counter at the store would be willing to make such a sacrifice for you? Would you be willing to make that sacrifice for her?

Think about how complex this situation is. We spend our entire lives living as Christians so that we can ultimately leave this earth to be reunited with Christ in the comfort and eternal luxury of Heaven. Christ loved us enough to leave the comforts and luxuries of Heaven, to live a life of discomfort in the earth, and to make arrangements so that we might one day join Him back in Heaven. His sole purposes for coming to earth were to serve and to suffer. With that being said, it is absolutely no coincidence that Christ refers to the church [who He left and came for] as His bride. And He commonly refers to Himself as the Husband. In essence, He is giving us a clue as to how He desired for the husband to treat his bride, and for the bride to treat her husband.

One of the prerequisites of an effective marriage, as laid out for us in Genesis, is for the man and the woman to have the ability to leave home and cleave to one another. When Christ came to earth, He didn't just leave home, but He adapted to the cultures of the earth. He did things like wear clothes and eat food. He became a part of the culture, without losing His identity. You may be wondering how all of this speaks to relationships, but it does speak directly to relationships. If you are going to have successful relationships, you must at some point be willing to leave parts of you, your upbringing, and your culture behind. If Christ would have attempted to live exactly how He lived in heaven, He would have been ineffective, because there is no suffering in Heaven.

When He left Heaven and came to earth, He didn't come to make the journey about Him; He came to suffer and to make the journey about you and me. He left His home to serve us. Imagine how powerful and fulfilling your life would be if you left your home every day with the sole purpose of serving others, even if it meant that you would have to suffer. Imagine how amazing your relationship with your co-workers would be if you made it your mission to leave the comforts of your own logic, ideas, and thought processes to make sure that someone else's voice was heard, and their opinion taken into consideration.

When a man and woman come together in marriage, there must be a process of leaving and cleaving. The word leave means, *"to give up, abandon or forsake."* Cleave means, *"to split, separate, or fall apart."* If a man and a woman are going to become one flesh, there is a severing that must take place physically, and to a certain extent, emotionally. Not only are they severing ties with the family structure and the foundational structure by which they were rooted and nurtured in, but there are some ideologies that must be left behind when you are moving forward in relationship.

This is not to say that you must abandon every thought process and conviction that you have about relationships; but it does stand to reason that you cannot allow your ideas to be considered that law. When you are married, you become one with a new set of ideas, thought processes and approaches. Part of the suffering is when a person is required to exchange a new approach for a set way. Many marriages fail because neither party is willing to relinquish their right to be right. This leads to pride, and pride undoubtedly leads to a fall. The first ingredient in the recipe of successful marriage and relationships is the willingness to leave.

Cleave means to split or separate. Often times, the suffering portion comes in the separation process. When my wife and I got married, we both struggled with this. She struggled with no longer having her father be her first recourse when she had problems. I was now that first recourse. I struggled with being raised an only child, and being accustomed to always having things my way. It is when we made these adjustments that we began seeing an extreme difference in the health of our marriage. Are there areas that you need to leave behind?

Love

The second key ingredient is love. Love is a very complex word, yet it is simple when understood and applied. There are some misconceptions about love that we must clear up before we move any further. Many have classified love by what they have heard in a song, or seen on a television show. And while these may be the results of loving relationships, they in no way, shape or form bring meaning to the word love. There are many that, if asked to describe love, would give wonderful attributes but would not give the definition. It would be robbery of we attempted to move any further without giving a clear and concise definition for love.

There are four Greek words for love, and they are distinguished by usage. Let's take a look at these ancient Greek definitions for the word love:

Agape means ***love*** (unconditional) in Modern day Greek. In Ancient Greek, it often refers to a ***general affection*** or ***deeper sense of true love***.

Eros is a passionate love, with sensual desiring and longing. The Modern Greek word ***erotas*** means ***intimate love***.

However *eros* does not have to be sexual in nature. *Eros* can be interpreted as a love for someone whom you love more than a brotherly love. *Eros* is where get our modern day word *erotic* from.

Philia means *friendship* or *brotherly love* in Modern Greek. It includes loyalty to friends, family, and community. It is where we get the name Philadelphia, which is commonly known as the city of brotherly love.

Storge means *affection* in both Ancient and Modern Greek. It is natural affection, like that felt by parents for offspring.

As you can clearly see, love can at times be quite complex and can often be easily misunderstood. Think of how many homes have been broken because what appeared to be an agape love ended up being eros? And how many families have been destroyed because of a lack of storge in the home? I can only imagine the neighborhoods that have suffered at the hands of violent men and women who have not been taught the concept and the significance of storge. On the same token, if we are going to have relationships that are founded on Christ, we must walk in all four of these types of love and exhibit them in our everyday affairs.

As we are examining John 3:16, it's befitting that we point out the exact type of love that is being presented in the text. The word love in this particular portion of scripture speaks to an agape love. It is the type of love that extends beyond condition. In thinking of a God that loved the world that He made a decision to give His only Son, one could only imagine how beyond condition that love would have had to have been. (Not sure what you want to say here.) In essence, you could exchange that word world for enemy. God loved even His enemies so much that He rendered the thing that He cherished as a sacrifice for that very enemy. Now that is some love. Let's look at how this speaks to our relationships with those that surround us.

It's a wonderful thing to express that we love one another, but it is a completely different thing to prove it. It's sad to say that there are many that have based their commitment on mere expressions of love, and not examples of love. Imagine what kind of trouble we would be in had Christ only expressed his love for us, but had not exemplified it by dying on the cross for us. It is easy to love those that are loveable, but it can at times take great effort to love those that are not loveable. The interesting thing is that we never read where Christ struggled with having an agape love, even for His enemies. Let's take it a step further. Christ referred to us as His bride, even when were unworthy of the title. He died for His bride, even when we were unworthy. He rose again for His bride, even when we were unworthy.

Here is the bottom line. The success rate is guaranteed if we allow Christ and His relationship to His bride, to be the blueprint by which we build our love for one another. We can't expect to build a lasting marriage on eros, phileo, or storge. It takes an agape love to overlook shortcomings, failures, misunderstandings, disagreements, temperaments, and mistakes. We understand that true marriages aren't short sprints, but they are marathons. It becomes quite difficult to win in the marathon of marriage if you are unprepared to go the distance. Real, agape love, can turn a mediocre marriage into an exceptional one. It can transform a simple friendship into an extraordinary friendship. The most important thing to remember about an agape love is that it can never be about you, it has to always be about who it is towards, without condition.

Give

Before we go any further, let's take a brief look at the ingredients that we have thus far. We learned how in every
successful marriage there must be a leaving and cleaving.
We've also briefly identified and expounded on the need
for every successful relationship to have an unconditional
love to strengthen and sustain it. I want to now look at the
third ingredient that causes a marriage to succeed. If we
are going to experience the depth in our marriages that
God desires for us to experience, giving has to be a way of
life. What's even more interesting is that it is impossible to
separate love from giving. It has been said time and time
again, love isn't love unless it's given away. Giving is the
mechanism by which love is transmitted. The greatest example of this concept is put on display for us to learn from
in John 3:16. God's response to him loving the world was
to give. What a wonderful pattern for us to glean from and
follow in our relationships.

Not only do love and giving go hand in hand, but they also
share in complexity. Giving, if not defined, can be completely misunderstood. And if it can be misunderstood, it
can be mishandled. Have you ever had someone give you

something, and then later they asked for it back? That has happened to me on numerous occasions, and it quite discomforting every time that it happens. It's unsettling because there almost appears to be a breach in the contract that doesn't really exist. There is a word that describes what happens in scenarios like that. It's called lending. Many have received what they considered gifts that were in reality loans. And many have yielded with intent of giving, only to ask for it back because they realized that they really didn't have it to give in the first place. Were you aware that this happens in relationships all of the time? But, I am not talking in reference to money or any other tangible item. I am referring to love. It's quite possible to lend love, instead of giving it away.

To give in essence means to turn over the possession or control of something without cost or exchange. We recognize that love is merely just a word, until it is given away. We also now understand that to give means to expect absolutely nothing in return. If a person is expressing their love toward another, yet they expect an expression of love in return, we have to ask ourselves if it's really love that we are giving in the first place. We never read where God loved enough to loan us his Son. He loved, and then He proved His love with a gift. What's even more powerful is that He was fully aware of the fact that many would reject the gift, yet He gave it.

Winning marriages occur between two people that are willing to give, yet failing marriages are between two people that are driven by their sense of entitlement. But in order to rectify the problem of giving, we must first evaluate why it is a struggle for people to give. Whether we are referring to giving our time, talent, treasure, or even emotions, people often hesitate to give because they view giving as loss. Most people are not willing to sacrifice where there is no gain. I have spoken with countless couples that have found themselves in trouble because one or both parties feel like there is no reciprocity for the love that they give. But, what they are really saying is, they haven't got a return on their investment. As long as you view love as a loan or an investment, you are setting yourself and the relationship up for failure.

Consider the concept for a moment. If I am constantly lending my wife love, it means I am constantly placing a demand on that love back. And, if she is constantly bogged down with the thought of repaying the loan, then she's never afforded the opportunity to store up love for me. And if one or both of us are emotionally bankrupt at any given time, our marriage is essentially devoid of love and quite destitute. If we are going to win at love, our thought process has to shift from the **how much can I get** theory, to the **how much can I give** school of thought.

Have you ever told someone that you love them, and become angry when they didn't express that they love you too? Have you ever been on the other end of an "I love you," and you didn't respond with "I love you too," only to have the lender of love get upset with you? Have you ever done someone a favor, for the sake of getting a favor in return in the near future? Has someone ever done something for you out of love, only to discover that it was love on loan? The truth is, if we are going to give declare our love for one another, we must learn to do so with no strings attached. Love is most powerful when it is given, and expects absolutely nothing in return. I want to see you succeed in your marriages and relationships, but if you are going to succeed in them, giving has to become a lifestyle. For those of you that struggle with giving, it is something that must be practiced, and you must be challenged on. You can start by saying I love you to a loved one without expecting it in return. Give your favorite book, Bible, or your coffee money away to a complete stranger, without any expectations attached. When you have mastered giving, you have mastered love. Go give!

Serve

The fourth and final ingredient in the recipe to a successful marriage is servitude. To leave is to love, and to love is definitely to give. You cannot give without having a heart to serve. Service is the last ingredient on purpose, and that is because it is the substratum to the entire recipe. The foundation of leaving, loving, and giving is service. The three of those ingredients funnel into one main ingredient called service. Relationships, whether between strangers or lovers, have the greatest success rate when those involved have a heart and a desire to serve one another. To a wife, there is no greater man in the world than a man that is willing to be her servant. The same goes for the husband. To him, there is no greater woman in the world than a wife that is willing to serve him. The key word is willing. There is a huge difference between a duty, and a service.

When a person is at your service, it means that they have yielded themselves to be used or they are useable. It's literally a person that is sent or employed to meet your specific need, as it relates to that institution. When you go to the fine hotel downtown, the door man is employed to serve you and your every need while you are a patron at that particular institution. The waiter at your favorite restaurant was hired to meet your dining needs, and to be of complete service to you. Even when you go to the movie theatre, the ticket masters sell you your ticket while the ushers direct you to your exact theatre. They were interviewed and selected, because they exemplified the skills that were desired for the service that was expected at that establishment. Is it possible that God has selected you especially to be of complete service to your spouse or loved one?

Christ left the comfort of Heaven to come into the Earth to love and to serve us, by giving His life as a sacrifice. He did that because He loved us, yet at the same time He desired to set the ultimate example of servitude for us. Nothing about what He did for us was ever about Him. His leaving, His loving, His giving, and even His serving were for and about us. He didn't do it so that He could get accolades, because the truth is He was despised. He didn't do it for what He could gain, because in all reality He lost His life. He didn't do it because we were that worthy; to be quite frank, Christ was the innocent One and we were guilty. He did it because He has a heart to serve His bride. He endured the ultimate suffering and sacrifice, and He never once complained. I hate to admit it, but I have been asked to make much lesser sacrifices for my bride, and I complained from the start to the finish.

The essence of service is putting others first. It says *you first, then me*. Self servitude, on the other hand, says *me first, and whoever else can fit after me*. What is most unfortunate is that many of us serve others in our career, yet we refuse to serve those that we claim to love the most. Christ structured the institution of marriage to be nurtured and supported by acts of service, not sessions of love making. It's a wonderful thing to say that you love someone, but an even more powerful thing to express it through service.

I have spent many years teaching on service, and there are three key components that I have found make a great servant. Those attributes are called the **Triple-A Method of Service [TAMOS]**:

1. **Anticipation**: It is important that a good servant has the ability to anticipate the need, even before there is a need.

2. **Acceleration**: Once the need has been assessed, it must become a priority.

3. **Action**: The key to great service is the ability to get the job done in a timely manner, and in excellence.

Anticipation coupled with acceleration and action makes for a fail proof plan for quality service. I want you to imagine how exhilarating a marriage would be if each spouse began practicing the Triple-A Method of Service? Whenever I counsel couples, I encourage them to get into the habit of out-serving each other. I teach them to make it their responsibility to beat each other to the punch, in relation to servitude. When this happens, both couples experience the highest level of fulfillment, both from being served and having the ability to serve. I want to encourage you to begin making it a habit of out-serving your spouse. The key is to do it without expecting anything in return.

When serving your spouse, always keep in mind that you are to serve them the way they desire to be served, not the way that you would desire to be served. This requires a great deal of dialogue, asking of questions, and personal observation. The thing that you cannot do is allow yourself to get frustrated when they express that you may not be meeting the need. Remember, service is ultimately about making sure that the customer is satisfied with the product.

Consider your spouse your customer: What are you going to do to serve them until they are satisfied?

CHAPTER FIVE

Healed Without Scars

Matters of the Heart

I have spent many years of my life working in the medical field, and in the operating room to be specific. I have seen a myriad of tragedies occur, as well as my share of happy endings. I have seen people come in the hospital on the brink of death, and walk out of the hospital full of life. I have seen people come in full of vigor, and end up lying on their back for several months with unexpected diagnoses. What I find most interesting are the people that I have seen that have lived with their condition for so long, that they no longer notice it.

I can recall a patient that came into the O.R. for surgery that had literally half of his face missing. 90% of the right side of his face had been eaten away by cancer. The wonderful thing about his story is that after several operations, they were able to repair the damage, and he survived the disease. What I find disheartening about his story is that he lived at home with his wife and family, and no one was caring enough to bring him in to get his deteriorating face taken care of. The longer that they waited, the worse it got. It reached a point that he was in serious jeopardy of losing his life. And to think that the people that he was with everyday, and claimed to love him, wouldn't intervene in the situation to get him help. I have seen it time and time again, that those families that surround sick people become desensitized to the sickness, and it literally begins to go unnoticed over time.

As you can imagine, that gentleman had formed his life-style and habits around his sickness and his appearance. He wore masks and sunglasses to his appointments. He wore hoods and scarves in public, and every type of weather, all of this to disguise his sickness. You might be wondering what this has to do with relationships, but it has every-thing to do with them. There are many of us that have places in our hearts and emotions that are deteriorating, and we won't do anything about it. We have become the masters of disguise, finding ways to hide and cover up the emotional sickness that has become a cancer in our hearts. We have become our own personal physicians, formulating our own diagnosis, and prescribing our own remedies. If the truth were told, I can honestly say that I had suffered for many years of a broken and cancerous heart.

I'd allowed things like fatherlessness and abandonment to become a cancer in my heart. I spent many years responding to that void in my heart, by doing things that were destructive to me and those that were involved with me in those seasons of my life. I'd spent many years going from one relationship to another, seeking stability in relationships. I'd gone from one sex partner to another, seeking emotional balance in a place and people that couldn't bring that balance. I'd gone from drinking to drugs, seeking to fill the void that was in my heart. I was love sick, and couldn't seem to find the cure. I'd hurt one young lady to the next, simply because I was attempting to heal the hurt that was happening in my heart, by using my relationships and antidotes, but to no avail.

The thing that I find most bothersome is that I was actually desiring and seeking an authentic relationship. I believe that there are many that are reading this book that are where I was, seeking, yet unable to find. There are also those that have found, but are unable to manage. The issue wasn't that I didn't desire to be faithful and madly in love, because I did. The real issue was that, like many of you, there were a thousand little holes in my heart that hindered me from having and holding on to something genuine.

Although there were many that witnessed the man's face deteriorating and rotting away, there wasn't a person in the world that could convince him that he needed serious help. He had to come to that resolve within himself. He had to take a long look in the mirror, and make the decision that his life was too valuable for him to be stuck in the prison of his fears.

I encourage you today to examine closely the patterns of your heart. There is a reason why we do everything that we do, and the more aware we are of the reasoning behind our actions, the more prepared we are to make the necessary changes. Don't let the negative matters of your heart out shadow the positives. Don't allow what didn't go right in your past hinder what could, should, and would go right in your future. It was never God's desire for us to love with a limp. His desire is for us to live prosperous lives, even as it speaks to our love lives. Take along hard look in the mirror of your heart and determine that you will confront those issues that need to be confronted, and correct those things that need to be corrected. Your heart will thank you for it.

Healed With No Scars

It's often difficult to comprehend the idea of Adam and Eve were at one point in their life single, but they were. Not only were they single, but they were successfully single. They lived lives that were pleasing to God, and God in return took great pleasure in rewarding them with one another. I know that it is probably hard to wrap your mind around the idea of Adam and Eve being single, because for one, the Bible doesn't say a lot about their lifestyle as a single man and woman of God. The second reason that we often have a hard time grasping the concept of them being single is because we clearly understand that from the time of their conception, they were made for each other. Subconsciously we rush to put them together, rather than placing a microscope on their lives as singles, so that we can learn of them. There are three key factors that I want to direct you to as it relates to their lives as single man, and single woman. Those three key factors are ***the process, the preparation,*** and ***the presentation.*** They were successful in pleasing God as a singles because of their process, preparation, and their presentation. We will spend some time now investigating these three words in comparison to the lives of Adam and Eve.

The Process

In order to understand the process, we must first understand the concept that mankind were spirit beings before they were natural beings. You and I have always existed in the heart and mind of God. Even before He chose to present you to the world through your birth, he knew who you would be, what you would be, and who would walk through this life with you. You were in existence from beginning, and He chose a special day, your birthday, to bring you from the invisible unseen spirit realm, into the visible seen natural realm. God did this because he had a specific plan and purpose that He desired to fulfill through your life in the earth. Your existence in the earth is intentional, and by no means a mistake. In order to get you here from the spirit realm, he took you through a process called child birth. You were born for greatness.

Anytime that God used someone great in the Bible, He took them through a personal process to get them to greatness. Jesus is the ultimate example of process, as he endured a great and terrifying process to make sure that we experience an eternity with Him in Heaven. It's safe to say that many of us want the promise, yet we are not willing to endure the process that comes along with it. Yet, much of the character and integrity that is needed to keep the promise is developed in the process. Adam and Eve went through a process while they were single that literally lead them directly to the promise, which was each other.

We read in Genesis 2:7 that, *"the Lord God formed man of the dust of the ground, and breathed into his nostrils the breath of life; and man became a living soul."* That word *formed* when translated from the original Hebrew translation means *distressed.* Distressed means *in need of immediate help.* This is critically important, because in Genesis 2:18, the Lord said, *"It is not good for man to be alone; I will make him and helpmeet for him."* It's interesting that as God took Adam through the process of being formed, He placed inside of him the need for a helper. There was never a moment in Adam's life that he was not in need of a help meet, because the need for immediate help was a part of his DNA.

It's important for every single person reading this to understand that Adam's promise was locked inside of his process. He could have never received his promise, had he not endured the process. Don't lose sight of what the process was for Adam. It was him being formed by God. When God formed Adam, he was simply shaping and molding Adam into the man that He envisioned Adam to be. Adam could not get his Eve until God had finished making him who he needed him to be, for his Eve. I need every single man that is reading this to know that if you are still single, he is not finished processing you. I charge you to take full advantage of what He desires to do in, on, and through you while you are single, so that when your promise comes, you don't contaminate her because you are undone on the inside.

Adam wasn't the only one that endured a process. We read in Genesis 2:22, *"And the rib, which the Lord God had taken from the man, made He a woman, and brought her unto the man."* When you take a close look at this scripture, you will discover that just like Adam, Eve went through a process herself. Notice that the scripture said that she was made, rather than formed. The word *made* in the original Hebrew translation means *built up* or *skillfully formed.* It sounds as if God made some special adjustments when He was fashioning the woman. She endured the building process, in order that she might be well prepared to help Adam fulfill the vision and plan that was placed in him. I must pause here long enough to say that many single men and women hinder themselves from getting to the promise, because they aren't willing to patiently endure the process. The process is the prerequisite to the promise.

The Preparation

I can recall many years ago when my wife and I first met, I devised a plan to impress her with my culinary skills. I decided to invite her over for dinner, where I'd planned to cook this elaborate dinner for her. The dinner consisted of a pasta dish, salad, fried chicken, and of course dessert. I was able to complete the entire meal just in time, as she arrived while everything was still hot. I must admit, the salad looked quite fresh, the pasta had just the right amount of sauce, and the fried chicken was a nice golden brown. [Disclaimer: I had never fried chicken before]

As we sat down to eat, she complimented me on how good the food looked and smelled. I was excited for her to taste this masterpiece of a meal. As she took a bite of her chicken, she had the most interesting look on her face.

Her statement, "My chicken is bleeding inside," matched the look of despair on her face. Sure enough, as I took the fork to peel away the skin on my chicken, it was bleeding inside as well. I must admit that this had to have been one of the most embarrassing moments of my life. Needless to say, I ended up reheating the grease, and cooking the chicken even further until it was all the way done.

The mistake that I'd made while cooking that meal was simple, I assumed that the inside was done, based on the appearance of the outside. Because of my lack of experience, and poor timing, I allowed my senses to override what was actually true. Have you ever made a judgment about a thing based on what was on the outside? Have you ever bought a product based on the box? Have you ever made a decision to enter into a relationship with someone simply based on the exterior, without ever really examining what was going on within their heart, mind, and soul? If the truth were told, we've all bought the box at one point or another in our lives. We've all misjudged people's character and intents based on our own assumptions. Let's take that school of thought even further. Many of us have made incorrect assumptions about ourselves, simply because we started believing that we were actually the person that we dress up and portray ourselves to be in the company of others. We have often had the proclivity to believe our own press when in reality, underneath it all is a person that is bleeding on the inside.

Although the chicken that I'd prepared was golden brown and smelled good, it had not gone through the complete process, and was therefore toxic. I believe that if we were to investigate and identify the root cause of most toxic relationships, we would find that these are relationships where either one or both parties are emotionally undone and bleeding on the inside. That comes as a result of not allowing themselves to be healed and processed from past hurts and pains. What I find even more common is that many of these people go from relationship to relationship, seeking fulfillment and healing from the relationship, rather than from God. There are few things that are worse for a relationship than emotionally infected people.

In dealing with mathematical equations we understand that two halves make a whole. When you speak to relationships and marriage in particular, your success rate is heightened when two wholes unite to make a whole. A broken man and a broken woman can never expect to experience wholeness in their relationship. A whole man and a broken woman can't expect to experience complete wholeness in the relationship. Neither can a whole woman and a broken man expect to experience wholeness in the relationship. The only place that complete wholeness is guaranteed in a relationship is when it's a relationship between two spiritually and emotionally whole people.

Luke 14:28 (KJV) asks, "***Which of you, intending to build a tower, sitteth not down first, and counteth the cost, whether he have sufficient to finish it?***" What a profound question. I can recall the many hours of talking and planning that it took for my wife and I to plan our wedding. We spent hours crunching numbers, adding and subtracting people from our lists, and even calculating hours of overtime that we would have to work to meet our budget. If we were to be completely honest, we spent more time counting the cost of our wedding than we did counting the cost of being married. We didn't really talk in detail about how our emotional past would affect our future. We didn't discuss how the letdowns in our lives, at the hands of others, would affect the way we might treat each other. We never really discussed how our skewed view of the marriages that we had seen might one day affect how we view our own marriage. As a man, I never really counted the cost of how the hurt from my fatherless past might affect my future relationships with my own children. We spent a great deal of effort preparing for everything else but our emotional future together. The sad thing is that like us, hundreds of thousands of couples make this same mistake every year. And, hundreds of thousands of half men and half women get married every year, hoping that the union would somehow and someway make them whole. There is only one tried and true person that can stop the internal hemorrhaging, and that person is Jesus Christ. Make the decision today to allow God to make you whole for your future of love.

The Presentation

It's safe to say that processes and preparations are the tools by which we as individuals are matured and developed. We learn about faith and prayer during the process and preparation stages of life. We learn about endurance and long suffering during these trying times. Our temperance and humility is developed while we are being processed and prepared. Your process and preparation will teach you who you are. The process and the preparation lead you to the presentation. It is to life, what school is for education. It is the vehicle by which you grow in depth, knowledge, and maturity. You cannot graduate high school until you have completed or tested out of the twelfth grade. You cannot get to the twelfth grade until you have completed or tested out of the eleventh grade. Your processes set you up for your presentation. Many who are reading this book right now are still single. I want to encourage you to allow God to completely process and prepare you for marriage, so that you aren't toxic at the time of presentation.

We are given a wonderful example of this in Genesis chapter two, as the Lord is getting ready to present Adam's promise to him. In Genesis 2:21-22, we see what the transition from preparation to presentation looks like. If you blink, you might just miss it. But, if you open your eyes to the revelation of what took place, it will revolutionize your life. The Word says, ***"And the Lord God caused a deep sleep to fall upon Adam, and he slept: and He took one of his ribs, and closed up the flesh instead thereof. And the rib which the Lord God had taken from man, made He a woman, and brought her unto the man."*** Here we see both Adam and Eve being processed and prepared.

What is most exciting is to be afforded the opportunity to witness God the Father, who'd arranged this marriage, present a spotless woman to a spotless man. There is a prerequisite in the text that leaps out as us, and it is found in the last stanza of verse 21, when it says, "***and closed up the flesh instead thereof***."

Why are these six simple words so important? What they show us is that God was so concerned about the health of this marriage that he refused to present the bride to her husband until he had been healed and made whole. God put Adam to sleep [administered the first anesthesia]; opened him up and extracted the rib [performed the first surgery]; closed him up and woke him up [took him through rehab and recovery]; and united him with his bride [performed the first wedding]. But, He wouldn't allow the wedding to take place until He had taken the time to heal Adam.

This is vitally important because He understood the state that the man, woman, and relationship would be in had He not decided to heal him. There are four key things that would have undoubtedly occurred in that relationship had God not healed the man first:

1. The woman would have spent her entire life nursing the man's wounds. Unfortunately, we see this pattern today with men that are unable to cope emotionally. Many of them spend their entire lives expecting women to nurse their wounds, and stroke their emotions. When a man doesn't allow God to process him completely, he often looks to the women in his life [mother, girlfriend, sister, friends, and wife] to undergird him emotionally. This in essence cripples him even further and prevents proper emotional balance and psychological growth.

2. The man would have spent his entire life making excuses for himself, as to why he is not the man that she expects him to be. Many broken men contract what I call the "woe is me" virus. They would often much rather make excuses than make changes. When God took the time to heal Adam, He took all ownership off of Himself and placed it all on Adam.

3. Had God not healed Adam, he would have become an infection in the marriage and in the family.

When we look at that state of our families today [in western culture], it is quite evident that we are dealing with a generation of hurting men and infected families. The Lord has required the man to be the head of the household. What affects the head will eventually affect the body. What infects the head will eventually hinder the forward mobility of the body. A broken man is a virus waiting to happen. A healed man is a remedy waiting to happen.

4. Had Adam not been healed, he would have spent his entire life covering up and medicating the broken area of his life. When a person is broken, they often have the proclivity to secretly medicate the brokenness. This would have been a huge distraction for Adam and Eve in their marriage, and it becomes a huge distraction for many today. We medicate with drinking, drugs, pornography, overeating, physical and emotional abuse, crime, and so many other things that are ungodly. The real cure is the healing power of Christ.

We have heard it said a million times over, one bad apple can spoil the whole bunch. That statement is not only true, but can be applied to relationships as well. One rotten heart has the propensity to change the dynamic of an entire household, and even an entire family. Just as God did not present Adam to Eve until he was healed, we too should seek that same wisdom and outcome for our lives. Our prayer should be, *"**Lord heal me, so that I am not toxic to those that come into contact with me.**"* When you pray that prayer, God is waiting with open arms to heal you and mend you where you are broken. Your wholeness is simply a prayer away.

Emotional Band Aids

Contrary to popular belief, a new relationship is not the cure for a past hurt. Hurt people often have the inclination to use new relationships as emotional band aids. The major characteristic of a Band-Aid is that is a topical treatment. Band-Aids are non-medicinal, and they do not administer any remedies. Their primary function is to cover and protect the scar. If we were to be completely honest, the best way to allow a scar to heal is to expose it, and not to cover it.

New relationships can function as emotional Band-Aids because they have the same characteristics as a Band-Aid.

They are very surface, they are not the remedy, and in them we tend to cover and protect what's really going on beneath the surface. When we spend our entire lives covering and protecting our ego and emotions, we never allow people the opportunity to discover who we actually are. When we meet them, they actually meet the Band-Aid, rather than meeting the real us. There are many that get engaged and even go so far as getting married, and all the while they're hiding deep-rooted hurts and pains under the Band-Aid of the relationship. It is in many cases the constant friction of the marriage that forces the Band-Aid off, and allows the deep-rooted scars to be exposed.

I encourage every person that is reading this to examine yourself emotionally. Are there things that you need to address that can be detrimental to your relationship? Are there emotions that have been tucked away in the safe treasure chest in your heart that need to be unearthed and addressed? Are there things that you haven't been honest with even yourself about? Perhaps you need to come clean with yourself or with someone else that has hurt you. Whether you are married or not, I encourage you to confront your emotions, and allow the healing power of the Lord to minister healing and wholeness to your life.

Hoarders

One of my favorite shows on television is Hoarders. The show highlights pathological or compulsive hoarders. A pathological or compulsive hoarder is one that acquires and stores things, often to offset an emotional imbalance. While hoarding is characterized by a physical action, the essence of hoarding is psychological. The root cause can often be traced back to a traumatic emotional experience that occurred earlier on in a person's life. The word "hoarder" is often synonymous with the word clutter, simply because hoarders tend to bury themselves in clutter. I've even witnessed hoarders that have had pets that they loved dearly get lost and die in the mounds of clutter, without the owner ever noticing that the animal is missing.

One of the things that I find most interesting about a hoarder is their innate ability to mask their disease. You may work with a hoarder and never even know it. You may even have a hoarder in your family and be completely unaware of it. The reason being, hoarders tend to take better care of themselves than they do their living spaces. In most cases, the problem isn't that the hoarder isn't well kept, but that they have trouble keeping order in their environments.

You may be reading this, and wondering why I am discussing hoarders right now. The truth is, there are many that are reading this book right now that are emotional hoarders. No, you don't have an issue with physical clutter, yet you have a huge issue with emotional clutter. You don't store things, yet you have a tendency to clutter your heart with negative thoughts and emotions. Most clutterers have a very difficult time allowing people to come into their homes, simply because they are afraid of being judged by the way that they have managed their living space. In many cases, the clutter is a physical representation of the psychological garrison that has been constructed, to separate the hoarder from the pain of the emotional trauma that they have experienced.

The emotional hoarder's sickness can manifest itself in tantrums, arguments, blaming, shouting matches, fighting, and even distancing themselves from people or circumstances. People that are hoarding or harboring pain of traumatic emotional experiences tend to use their outbursts and/or anger as a defense mechanism. It works as a defense mechanism by keeping people from getting too close to them. It protects them from having the covers removed, and from having their emotional vulnerabilities exposed. Do you know an emotional hoarder? Are you an emotional hoarder? It may be time to clear the clutter. Let's take a look at 7 practical tips to clear the emotional clutter of your heart, and find the liberty to love and trust again:

1. **Pray.** There is absolutely nothing that is impossible for God to do through you, for you, and by you. Ask God to rid your heart and thoughts of everything that is not like Him. Invite Him into your heart to be the balm that will mend and heal your brokenness. As you are seeking the Lord for your healing, make sure that you ask God for the wisdom and the patience that it will take to conquer your emotional giant. Most importantly, seek the Lord for courage to combat the fear that may attempt to arise and deter you from moving forward.

2. **Admit it**. If you are going to get the victory over your emotional clutter, you first have to admit that there is a problem. You will never have the capacity to fix what you don't have the courage to admit. Some will find this more difficult than others to do, but at the end of the day it is vitally necessary

for you to experience a healthy and whole heart. Admitting it simply means making the bold confession that there are some things in your heart that are unhealthy, and that you are going to allow yourself the time to address the problem with wisdom and patience.

3. **Confront it**. You will never conquer what you aren't willing to confront. Clearing the clutter of your heart takes the same effort as clearing the clutter of a room. You must be willing to confront the task at hand. Often times, facing the giant is the most difficult part of the battle. If you can pull yourself to the battle field, you have already done what is takes to win.

4. **Start where you are.** Rome wasn't built in a day, and neither are the emotional barriers that we build in our hearts. The seeds of many of the emotions that we feel were planted in our hearts at an early age. Many have walked around with these emotions embedded in their hearts for years. What is even more saddening is that there are negative experiences that are compiled on top of

negative experiences, and the emotions from those experiences are piled on top of one another.

5. **Dig it up at the root.** We often spend many years medicating the symptoms, rather than alleviating the root cause. The cough is not the cold; it's a symptom of the cold. The sneeze is not the cold; it's a symptom of the cold. Likewise, the alcoholism is not the problem; it's the symptom and byproduct of a much greater emotional problem. The adultery is not the problem; it's simply the result of a much greater emotional problem. The best way to get rid of the problem totally is to dig it up at the root. You can identify the root of your emotional problems by asking yourself the following questions:

    - When you are acting inappropriately (physically, verbally, or emotionally), what is the feeling that you have right before you act that way (lonely, tired, frustrated, depressed, angry, etc.)?

    - Are there particular people that trigger negative emotional responses in your life (father, mother, ex-companion, husband, wife)?

- Are there particular environments or places that cause you to reflect and respond negatively?

- Is there an experience, or a series of experiences from your past that have triggered negative emotional responses when you think of them?

- Is there a negative emotional experience that you have tucked away in the crevices of your heart that you have fought hard not to confront?

6. **Be restored.** One of the greatest mistakes that you could make after taking the time to confront the issues, is not allowing yourself time to be restored afterwards. It's like someone that has surgery on their leg. The doctor will instruct them not apply any unnecessary pressure to that leg until it is strong enough to support the body without being supported itself. The same goes for emotional healing. Your heart needs time to be healed and be strengthened, so that at some point it is strong enough to support itself. Take the time that you need to allow God to minister complete healing

and wholeness to you. Your heart will thank you for it later.

7. **Move forward.** Don't allow your past to paralyze your future. What is in the past should stay in the past, and you should never allow it stop you from moving forward. If people have mishandled you in the past, that simply means they weren't qualified to participate in your future. But, that does not give you an excuse not to have a future. Remember that the objects in the mirror are closer than they appear. Your past hurts and pains are a reflection away from being a reality, so keep your focus on your future and not your past.

CHAPTER SIX

Single and Sexy

The Reality of Sexuality

What do you do when you are single, saved, and want to have sex? Who do you talk to when you can't stop the desires of having an intimate sexual encounter? What do you do when your mind is telling you no, but your body is telling you yes? How do you handle problems with masturbation or wet dreams? How do you recover as a single person, when you have fallen into the snare of sexual temptation? These are real questions that warrant real answers. But, if the truth were told, these answers are hard to come by in the church.

This poses a major problem, because for many single Christians, sexual desires are a real reality. What's even more disturbing is that many Christian singles have been taught that sexual impurity is a sin, and something that they are to distance themselves from, yet very few of them are given real solutions. I recently read in an article published by Psychology Today that according to the *Kinsey Report (Sexual Behavior in the Human Male)*, 54 percent of men think about sex every day or several times a day, 43 percent a few times a week or a few times a month, and 4 percent less than once a month. What an alarming statistic. Over half of the men that were surveyed admitted to thinking about sex at least once a day, and many several times a day.

As I am writing this, it has caused me to reflect on my own days as a young single Christian man. I was born and raised in church, yet I can't ever remember hearing one single lesson about sexual purity. I remember hearing that sex was bad, yet they never taught us what was so bad about it [which, I still can't find an answer to that one]. They told us that sex wasn't something that we needed to be thinking about, yet they never taught us how to handle the thoughts when they did enter our minds. They told us that sex was something that you weren't supposed to talk about, yet they never taught us how to have mature conversations about the subject of sex.

I believe that when a person is misinformed about any-thing, they are susceptible to misuse that which they are misinformed about. If a person is never taught about sex, they will undoubtedly mishandle the sexual situations that are presented to them. If one is not made aware that there is a Godly perspective by which sex should be viewed, they will often view it from the perspective that is most readily available to them. It stands to reason that skirting around the subject of sex doesn't make it any less real. I am in contact with single Christians everyday that can attest to the reality of sexual desires and temptations. Like any other problem, it doesn't just disappear when you ignore it. The question is, what are we going to do about it?

There must be some practical tools that we can give to Christian singles to empower them to live fulfilled lives of sexual purity. There has to be some instruction that follows the mandate. It is one thing to tell someone to fish, and an entirely different thing to show them how to fish. It is one thing to tell singles not to have sex, but it is something completely different when you show them how to position themselves to succeed at sexual purity.

I want every single man and woman that is reading this to know that you are not alone in your struggles. There are millions of single Christians all over this world that are confronted with sexual desires on a daily basis, many of which have fallen to those temptations and desires. You may be one of the ones that have fallen. Take confidence in knowing that failure isn't final, and as long as you have breath in your body, you have another chance. For those of you that have not fallen, but are contemplating it, you aren't alone either. I commend you for sticking to your guns, and holding out, even when it gets difficult at times.

Take courage in knowing that I was where you are. I understand the battle that you often face in your thoughts, and even in your body. I am fully aware of the turmoil that you can often find yourselves in on whether or not you have what it takes to fully live for Christ or whether you will succumb to the temptations that are before you. You are not alone in the least bit, but I want to do my part to walk you through the crisis of sexual desire and temptation.

Denial has never been an effective answer to sexual temptation. The key to winning any victory is to practice until your weaknesses become your strength. The same goes for winning the battle over sexual temptation. It will take discipline and practice, but you will win the battle. Like any battle, positioning is vital. In this chapter, you will learn how to position yourself to be victorious in the battle against sexual temptation. Remember to start where you are, and finish where you desire to be.

Celebrate Your Sexuality

Your sexuality is something that is to be celebrated, and not depreciated. It is not something that should be tucked away and hidden for later, but it is something that is for the now. We have often made the common mistake of confusing sex with sexuality, and they are two completely different things. We clearly understand that sexual intercourse is something that is shared between a husband and his wife, but sexuality speaks solely to the individual and the boldness and confidence that they walk in. One's sexuality is the assurance that they have in knowing who they are, and what they have to offer to the world and to a relationship.

Webster's New World College Dictionary describes sexuality is *the state or quality of being sexual*. Your sexuality speaks to your capacity for sexual feelings, or your sexual orientation. There is no specific age as to which one experiences their sexual awakening, although studies show that it often occurs during the preadolescent stage, in both boys and girls. A common response to this preadolescent sexual awakening is masturbation, by both boys and girls. It is safe to say that the majority of us, even as adults, have not been encouraged to confront and discover our sexuality, in a healthy and godly way. It is one of those things that we are encouraged to tuck away, and to not confront until the opportune time. But, our sexuality is who we are. It is because of sexuality that we are here in the first place, so why not talk about it?

Both sex and sexuality are important, and they complement each other. Much of the conflict and the confusion that occurs in the hearts and minds of Christian singles is their inability to differentiate between the two. It is possible to explore your sexuality without exploring sex. Not only is understanding your sexuality important, it is necessary to successfully graduate to the next level, which is marriage. Sexuality is one of those gifts of God that comes naturally, and rarely needs to be encouraged or forced. It is our sexuality that causes us to be attracted to one another. It is our sexuality that keeps us attracted to one another in the relationship, and in the courting relationship, and especially in the marriage.

A person can't fully understand themselves, until they have taken the time to discover their sexuality. As contrary as this may sound, the best way to establish sexual safeguards as a single person is to understand who you are as a sexual being. When you discover and gain an understanding of who you are, you essentially gain an understanding of what environments and situations are conducive to you living a victorious life as a single Christian.

Did you know that it was possible to be a sexual being, without having sex? Did you know that it was possible to be a sexual being, without compromising your faith or integrity? It's true. In order to understand that, you must first come to the realization that your sexuality is a gift from God that should be cherished and protected. It is the essence of your sexuality that will ultimately attract your spouse to you when they present themselves. The deep and spiritual response that we have been lead to believe is that there must first be a spiritual connection, before there is a physical connection. That couldn't be further from the truth. God delights in attraction and beauty. This is why he has given us the gift of sex drives and sexual appetites as well.

Sexuality is not merely in looks or body structure. It has everything to do with confidence, boldness, character, disposition, and personality. It's in how a person carries themselves, and presents themselves to the world. While it is not solely based on spirituality, there is something alluring about a person that has surrendered their life to the will of God, and is walking in His glory.

Before you can be a gift to anyone else, you have to understand that you are a gift to yourself. You have so much to offer yourself, and it is about time that you discover what that is. You celebrate your sexuality by rejoicing in the fact that you are a gift, and that you have so much to offer. The more that you discover who you are and what you have to offer, the less likely you are to waste your sexuality on meaningless and fruitless encounters and relationships. When God made you a sexual being, He placed something inside of you that was intended to be observed and admired by all, but experienced by only one.

Don't fight it, don't hide from it, and don't act like it's not important. Your sexuality is a big deal to God, and it should be a big deal to you. Walk in the boldness of knowing that God has given you something special for someone special. Until you get married, your sexuality should be reserved for your relationship with the Lord your God.

Winning Relationships

Show me your friends, and I will show you where you are headed. This couldn't be a more true statement. I would even go so far as to say, show me the top five people that you call the most in your phone, and I will show you your future. Who you surround yourself with is a clear indication of how successful or unsuccessful you will be. This is one of the leading principles that I learned and have lived by for many years now. Surround yourself with people that are where you desire to be, and one day you will be the person that somebody behind you wants to be surrounded by. Success begets success, and failure begets failure.

This same principle speaks to our intimate relationships. It is impossible to succeed in a relationship with someone that is headed in the opposite direction. The Bible calls this being unequally yoked together. A yoke is a tool that is commonly used to bind the necks of two oxen together to keep them moving in the same direction and working to obtain the same goal. It is virtually impossible to win in relationships that are counter-distinctive to who you are. This is why it is critically important to take careful consideration to who you allow yourself to be yoked with in relationships.

Later on in this chapter we will give practical tips on establishing boundaries, but it is important to note that boundaries are fruitless if the relationship is fruitless. One of the greatest mistakes that a single Christian can make is to establish a relationship with someone that is not going in the same direction as you are spiritually. It is also critical to note that being a Christian does not automatically qualify them to be your spouse. Not every single Christian is striving for sexual purity. You set yourself up for failure when you allow yourself to become serious in a relationship with someone that is willing to compromise their integrity and yours. If you are going to win, you must be willing to develop winning relationships.

The world watched with an undivided attention as star basketball player Lebron James announced that he was taking his talents from the Cleveland Cavaliers to the Miami Heat. Many were surprised to discover that James was leaving, not because he would be making more money, but because he desired to be a member of a winning team. He was willing to risk the scrutiny and criticism that would come as a result of him leaving, all to be considered a champion.

Please notice that James clearly understood that his ability to win was contingent upon his ability to be surrounded by those that have winning attitudes. He had a vision, mission, and a goal, and he made the sacrifices that were necessary to be on a winning team.

It is extremely important that singles position themselves to win in their season of singleness. They can position themselves to win by maintaining winning relationships. Winning relationships occur when two people have communicated their goals, and are working hard at making sure that each other's goals and values are being respected at all costs. It's safe to say that communication and mutual respect are probably the most important factors in assuring that there are continuous victories in the relationship. Winning relationships don't just happen, they take a great deal of effort and work.

Understand that it is merely impossible to win in a relationship with someone else, if you aren't winning in a relationship with yourself. I've come to understand that people that don't respect themselves generally lack the respect of others. People that don't value themselves are often devalued by those that come into contact with them. It is important to note that if you are going to demand the respect of others in a relationship, you must demand respect from yourself. The way to assure that you have a winning relationship yourself is to invest in your relationship with your Heavenly Father. What better person to have a winning relationship with than the one that values who we are, even when we aren't worth it?

When you make the investment in your relationship with Christ, and you allow His Spirit to make an investment in you, you become a great investment to someone else. Please know that winning relationships aren't just limited to love interests, but they speak to your relationships in general. When you respect yourself, you demand the respect of everyone around you, whether they are family, friends, or associates. Win with yourself, and you will win with others.

Lord Help Me; I Want To Have Sex

I want to speak directly to the Christian single right now. I won't waste time acting like sexual temptation isn't a reality for you, because I know that it is. I won't act like having the church tell you not to have premarital sex is the only safeguard that you need not to engage in sexual acts, because we know that's not true. I clearly recognize that sexual temptation is a very real struggle for you, and something that you deal with every single day of your lives. If we were to be quite frank, many of you want to have sex, and you want to have it bad. Many of you are having sex, and you want to stop. Many of you are having sex, and you once felt guilty about it, but the guilt has slowly slipped away each and every time that you had sex.

Many of you aren't having sex, but you are bound by pornography and masturbation. I am very much acquainted with these feelings and bondages, because I was once the single Christian that wanted sex, was having sex, and was bound by pornography. I was always taught that it was wrong, and was always told not to do it, but I was never given practical tools to control my desires. I wouldn't dare write a book to you, about you, without giving you applicable tools to help you overcome those desires. As we all know, lying to ourselves about our feelings doesn't change them. Taking a position in leadership at our church doesn't change the feelings either. Changing our phone number and shutting down our social network accounts is not the cure either. The cure starts with the heart, and ends in our members [flesh].

I want to give you 10 practical safeguards that you can apply to your life to overcome sexual temptation:

1. **Prayer.** If you are going to succeed in overcoming sexual temptations, you must have a healthy and active prayer life. Philippians 4:13 says *I can do all things through Christ which strengthens me.* There is absolutely nothing that you can't overcome through the prayer of faith. Prayer has the ability to change your heart, tame your flesh, fill every void, bring peace to the storm, and comfort you when you are lonely. You suffer the risk of failing when you have no prayer life, but you're guaranteed a victory when you have an active prayer life. Cover yourself in prayer.

2. **Guard your mouth.** In Genesis you were given creative power. When you speak, things happen. Take careful consideration of what you put in the atmosphere with your words. When you say things like "I'm feeling lonely", or "I'm going to get into some trouble tonight", you set yourself up for failure. Your words shape your environment. Your environment and your flesh are both waiting on you

to give them direction with your words. Remember that Proverbs 18:21 reminds us that the tongue has the power of life and death in it. What you say is what you will see. It's important that you allow Philippians 4:13 to be a part of your everyday speech.

3. **Guard your hearing.** What you hear will determine what your spirit will respond to. What your spirit responds to will determine what your flesh responds to. What your flesh responds to will determine whether or not you are pleasing to God, or pleasing to the devil. If you are going to overcome sexual temptation, what you are listening to has to be conducive to where you desire to go. This is why you have to be a steward of what conversations you are having, what kind of music that you are listening to, and what kind of advice that you are receiving from others. You will win the war on your flesh through faith. Remember, according to Romans 10:17, *faith comes by hearing, and hearing by the word of God.* You must feed your spirit the Word of God for your sexual appetites to be a reflection of the Word of God.

4. **Guard your vision.** Simply put, keep a close watch over what you allow your eyes to see. Your flesh desires to see things that feed the flesh. Things like pornography, sexually driven music videos, racy ads, or even skin tight jeans. You must make a decision that you are not going to allow your eyes to feed your spirit things that are not healthy. Mathew 5:29 says, ***"If thy right eye offend thee, pluck it out, and cast it from thee."*** Are we to actually pluck our eye out? Absolutely not. What He is instructing us to do is to starve ourselves of the things that cause us to be offensive to our Father. When you focus your attention on things that are of God, you strengthen your spirit to respond like God would respond.

5. **Guard your thoughts.** 2 Corinthians 10:4-5 reminds us that, ***"The weapons of our warfare are not carnal, but mighty through God to the pulling down of strongholds. Casting down imaginations and every high thing that exalts itself against the knowledge of God, and bringing into captivity every thought to the obedience of Christ."*** You have to train your mind to think God thoughts. We

are instructed to bring our thoughts into captivity. Sexual sins are always thoughts before they are actions. When you get your mind under subjection, your body will soon follow. The way that you cause your mind to be in subjection is to meditate on the Word of God. As you meditate on the Word of God, your mind becomes transformed. When there is a transformation in your thoughts, there will undoubtedly be a transformation in your actions. Free your mind, and the rest will follow.

6. **Connect with winners.** We spoke earlier about winning relationships. If you are going to succeed at overcoming sexual temptation, you must be in a relationship with someone who shares your same goal of being abstinent until marriage. Your likelihood of failure is enhanced when you attempt to maintain a relationship with someone that does not share your same values. It is important that you make very clear your desire to remain abstinent until marriage, and that the person that you are involved with has a clear understanding of that. The quickest route to failure in a situation like this is miscommunication. You must have winning

connections to have and maintain a winning relationship.

7. **Be honest with yourself.** It is important that you are honest with yourself about what you can and cannot handle. You need to know what turns you off and what turns you on. You need to be aware of what situations make you most vulnerable [alone, tired, certain movies, certain memories, etc.]. When you are honest about what you can't handle, you can afford the luxury of what you can handle. Being honest with yourself is one of the greatest safeguards to sexual temptation.

8. **Avoid the traps.** Be careful that you are not setting yourself and your partner up for failure by doing things that promote promiscuity. Avoid things like being alone [and especially at night] with your partner, and steer clear of sleeping in the same bed with one another. Be careful about being too revealing around one another and you should certainly avoid getting undressed in front of one another. Always remember that you are a gift to your future spouse. One of the most disrespectful things that you can

do is allow someone else to unwrap and handle a gift that does not belong to them.

9. **Be careful when touching.** While holding hands and walking arm and arm can be simple, and romantic, they often lead to lowered safeguards. Be careful about touching and caressing, as they tend to be gateways to immediate arousal. Avoid extended kisses and physical activity that may be inappropriate. Remember that compromising in the small things can often lead to big mistakes. One of the most difficult things to do is to back down and cool off in the heat of the moment.

10. **Communicate your feelings.** If you feel like you are becoming sexually aroused, or a situation is going too far, communicate that. Again, if you are with someone that respects, values, and shares your same passions, your openness should not pose a problem. You have a right to your feelings; and you have a right to have your feelings honored and respected. It is important that you are in a relationship with someone that you are free and open enough to communicate exactly how you feel. Whatever you do, speak up.

If you are a single person that struggles with sexual temptation, please know that you are not alone. I encourage you to make these safeguards a habit. I assure you that if you apply all ten of these to your life, you will not struggle with sexual temptation. Please notice that prayer is your number one tool. Without prayer, you will not experience maximized success in applying the other nine to your life. You can and you will win the battle against your flesh, but it is going to take constant effort and attention. The enemy is looking for an opening, and you can't afford to give him one.

Pray this prayer with me:

Father God, I thank you today for your Spirit that comforts me. Thank you for the blood that covers me. Thanks so much for your grace and mercy that follow me. It is you that has called me righteous and I thank you. Thank you for forgiveness of sins.

Lord, I confess that I have sinned in many areas of my life. I have even struggled sexually, and I ask your forgiveness. You know where I am, and you know that my heart desires to please you, but there are times when I miss the mark. Lord, I need your strength like never before to be victorious in the battle against my flesh.

I ask you to place your hand on my life like never before. Give me the grace to do what is right; not according to my desires, but according to yours. Help me live a victorious life of sexual purity. Give me the strength to abstain, even when I have the desire to give in. Be a reminder to me. Please allow your Spirit that lives in me to be the ultimate safe guard. Thank you now for the victory in my life, and my future spouse's life. It is in Jesus' name I pray. Amen.

Enjoying Abstinent Relationships

There has been a great deal of controversy about whether single Christians should or should not date. I will admit that I have vacillated in my opinion about the subject. We understand that dating and courting are two completely different things. A date is simply an arranged time that two or more people have set aside to spend time together. Courting, on the other hand speaks to exclusivity. It is a relationship in which two people have come together, with the common goal of ending in marriage. To be quite frank, I am not opposed to dating, as long as both parties involved have very clear understanding of where they are in the relationship.

The Bible does not speak to dating, and so there are no specific guidelines to how Christian singles should approach dating. It is often difficult to identify the characteristics of a healthy dating/courting relationship.

There are so many single Christians that have been left out in the dark about what a healthy dating/courting relationship should look and feel like. Many singles have gotten in trouble because they have attempted to approach their Christian relationships with a worldly approach. One of the greatest ways to set yourself up for failure is to be devoid of proper information. There is a correct way to approach the dating/courting relationship from a Christian perspective. Let's take a moment to identify 6 characteristics of a healthy Spirit-led dating/courting relationship:

1. **Friendship.** The key to a healthy marriage relationship as well as a dating/courting relationship is friendship. Married couples should be each other's best friends, and that friendship should begin to develop at the dating courting stage. A friend is a person that you know well and have grown fond of. It is often a person that is on the same side in trying situations. Friendship is one of the primary ingredients of marriage. Husbands and wives not only communicate as lovers, but they must com-

municate as friends. In a dating/courting relationship, it is important that a friendship is established before anything else is established.

2. **Communication.** Communication is critically important because as your relationship matures, there will be emotionally challenging situations that will require effective communication. As you begin to know one another, there should be a level of vulnerability between both partners in the relationship. There must be openness and a willingness to communicate your feelings. As the relationship progresses to marriage, things such as finances, sexual desires, and parenting decisions will require open and honest communication. It is important that these open and honest communication habits are developed, even from the beginning of the dating/courting relationship.

3. **Affection.** Affection is important in the dating/courting relationship. Affection has often been confused with something sexual, but it is not. Affection is an expression of fond feelings from one person to another. That expression can be in

words or gestures. Kind words go a long way in the relationship, as well as acts of service.

4. A compliment to a man often carried the same weight as a rose to a woman. Healthy growing relationships consist of two people that have a healthy affection for one another. While affection is developed over time, it is fuel to the relationship.

5. **Reliability.** Nobody wants to be involved with a flake. Reliability is essential in a dating/courting relationship in that there will undoubtedly come a time when an emotional reliability will be necessary. As you grow and mature together, there will be situations that arise in life that force you to lean on those around you that you know to be reliable. What greater person to rely on than the one that you are in a committed relationship with? When you are single, and seeking a dating/courting relationship, you desire someone that is a person of their word. You desire someone that you can rely on to call you when they said that they would call you, and be there when they said that they would. Those very characteristics transfer over into the

marriage relationship. Reliability is a must.

6. **Mutual and Outside Friends.** It sounds funny, but it is important that partners in a relationship have friends that are outside of the relationship. This is critical because in situations where this is not the case, there is often a heavier burden on one or the other partner/spouse to be everything for the other. Friends promote an individuality that is needed to maintain a healthy relationship. It is also very important that each partner is accepting of each other's friends. In many cases, there are often friends that were in the picture even before the two met. These friendships are actually quite vital to the health of the dating/courting relationship as well, as they allow for an outlet for each person to go to for discourse and interaction.

7. **Common Goals.** It is important that both people have expressed their dreams and goals, and that they agree to support each other in seeing these goals fulfilled. It is important that singles share this information from the start, as to not waste time with someone that is not going in the same direc-

tion or carries that same values as you do. As you are praying and seeking a mate, make sure that you are clear about who you are and where you are going, and that you are able to express that to your mate. This is important for the health of the relationship. As couples grow together, their corporate and individual goals change, and there must be a willingness to make the adjustments necessary to accommodate each other's goals. This is why it is critically important that common goals are expressed in the relationship.

8. **Clear Direction.** An understanding of where you are and where you desire to go is key to a healthy relationship. It is important that singles have the ability to have vision, and express what their ultimate goals are. These goals speak to those things that they desire as individuals, as well as those things that they desire as partners in a marriage relationship. It's been said that if you don't know where you are going, you will be sure to get there. That speaks even to the relationship dynamic. If you don't know what you desire and expect in a relationship, you will accept anything. You must

know who you are, where you are going, and how your future companion will fit into that vision.

There are far too many characteristics that can be listed, but I wanted to point out six that are often overlooked or never even thought of. Please keep in mind that as you begin to connect and grow together in your relationships, you will have the ability to define what you believe to be the most important goals and characteristics of a healthy relationship. I encourage you to make those discoveries while you are single, and even as you begin to make those important relational connections.

CHAPTER SEVEN

The Quality Mate

Higher Expectations

I was recently watching a documentary that highlighted some of the world's most popular tourist locations. These particular locations varied from remote islands to bustling city high-rises. While many of them appeared to be on the opposite end of the spectrum, they all had a common thread. This common thread is what causes people to travel great lengths, and to spend their hard earned money for the experience. The common thread is quality. I have come to discover that in many cases people are willing to make sacrifices for the sake of quality.

Merriam-Webster's Dictionary describes quality as "***the standard of something measured against other things of a similar kind***." It refers to "***fineness and excellence***." Excellence is simply having good qualities at a high degree. Quality is the thing that separates the good from the great. It is important to note that while quality relationships include appearance and presentation, they are not limited to those things. Quality relationships are those that fulfill our emotional and physical needs, and that enrich our lives. Many people pay more attention to the quality of their clothing than they do to the quality of their relationships. They expect a higher quality of service from the waiter at the restaurant than they do from the date that is sitting across from them at the table at the restaurant.

Quality Begins With You

I have seen it time and time again, unmarried men and women who find themselves in and out of unhealthy relationships. They seem to go from one fruitless relationship to the next without really getting to the root of the problem. In many cases the problem is much less about the people who they find themselves in relationship with, but rather, about the condition of their own hearts. When it comes to relationships, they will attract who you are, and not necessarily whom you want. In most cases, you will attract your dysfunction. The condition of your heart will determine the condition of your relationships. I often put it this way; you will attract whom your heart can handle. Broken relationships are often the result of one or both parties in the relationship suffering from a broken heart, and healthy relationships are the result of healthy hearts uniting. Quality relationships occur when both parties hold themselves to a higher standard; so to experience quality relationships, you must be in environments that promote quality and excellence.

Believe it or not, quality begins with you. This is why it is vitally important for you to monitor the condition of your heart, because the condition of your heart will determine the condition of your relationships. Proverbs 4:23 supports this truth when it states, "Above all else, guard your heart, for it is the wellspring of life." Guarding your heart doesn't mean that you are exclusive, but it means that you are selective. Quality relationships have the ability to strengthen your heart, while dysfunctional relationships have the potential to weaken your heart. There is only one person who can be held accountable for the quality of your relationships, and that one person is you. Only you can guard your heart, and only you can allow someone access to your heart.

To guard your heart means to pay careful attention to who you allow access to your feelings. It means to monitor who you share your deepest secrets with, and who you allow yourself to be vulnerable with. Your heart is the essence of who you are. Companies and institutions protect the quality of their brand because their brand is who they are. For many of these companies their hiring process requires that they select people who are willing to protect the quality of their brand. You have the same obligation to engage in relationships that protect the quality of who you are and what you represent.

Expectations, Exceptions and Excuses

If you've got to make exceptions and excuses for someone's character and lack of integrity in the relationship, you have to question whether it was God who sent them. Exceptions lead to excuses, excuses lead to settling, and settling leads to discontentment. A relationship founded on discontentment is one that is bound to end in destruction.

Please note that availability does not always equate to compatibility or qualification. Just because they are available doesn't mean that they are quality or qualified. This is why it is critical that single people have clearly defined standards in place for their lives. It is equally important that they allow those standards to serve as a compass directing them to relationships with like-minded people. Where there are standards you will also find depth, quality, excellence and worth. Where there are no standards you will find shallowness, lack of quality, mediocrity and worthlessness.

Quality is not equal to perfection. It is logical to require quality relationships but it is not logical to expect perfect relationships, because no one is perfect. You and I must be careful not to expect a level of quality in others that we aren't exhibiting yourself. This hypocrisy is an easy way to lose the respect of those with whom you are in a relationship.

When you have experienced quality, it often becomes difficult to settle for mediocre. This speaks to a wide array of things, including relationships. When someone or something is of a higher quality, it has the tendency to raise the level of your expectation. When the level of your expectation has been raised, anything that is substandard becomes quite noticeable. This speaks to relationships as well.

The Power of Selection

I have witnessed on many occasions people who have had their hearts broken because they ignored the red flags that they were noticing in their relationships. God gives us wisdom and discernment as an advantage over satan, to keep us from falling victim to his snares. Along with wisdom, the Lord gave mankind free will. At the essence of this free will is the ability to make decisions with or without the prompting and leading of Holy Spirit. This free will allows us to decide where we go, what we do, who we do it with, and how we do it. It is the same free will that allows us to select our mate.

When we don't allow Holy Spirit to guide us in the selection process of our mates, we suffer the risk of making one wrong decision that could have an adverse effect on the rest of our lives. It is a wonderful thing to have the power of selection, but an even greater thing to lean on the wisdom of God to guide us as we make our decisions.

Unmarried people often ask me if it is wrong to have a list of things that they require from a potential mate. There is no simple answer to that, as there are many factors that play a role in formulating such a list. The most important thing to consider is motivation. The thing that is motivating you to make the list is the thing that will control what is on the list. God knows exactly what He desires for our lives, so when we surrender our will to His, our list becomes His, and His list become ours. Do you see how that works? Matthew 6:33 reminds us to: "Seek first His (God) Kingdom and His righteousness, and all these things will be added unto you." What things is He referring to? The list that we generate in our hearts and minds that we desire for God to fulfill.

God desires that we experience quality relationships in every facet of our lives. Those relationships are established when we allow ourselves to be patient, flexible and led by Holy Spirit. Could we formulate our own lists? Sure we could. Is it a more safe and fruitful practice to allow God's will to override our own will? It sure is.

Quantity and quality are two completely different things. When a person has identified their worth (quality), they are often more content with being alone, as they aren't interested in compromising their value and worth at the hands of someone who can't appreciate their value and worth. On the other hand, a person of quantity is often content with experimenting in relationships until they find one that works for them. The one major problem with the quantity type is that in most cases there are casualties involved in the process, and God never intended for our hearts to be crash test dummies, or stunt doubles.

If you are unmarried and desiring a fruitful relationship, I encourage you to pursue quality rather than quantity and convenience. Please know that quality relationships are gems, and you must be willing to wait and not settle until you discover your particular gem. Frustration and impatience can cause you to become a person of quantity rather than quality. We serve a quality God who gives quality gifts to His quality children when they are patient enough to wait on them.

No Advertisement Needed

When was the last time you've seen a Bentley commercial on television? The reality is, you have likely never seen a Bentley commercial on television. Why is that? It is because Bentley is afforded the opportunity to spend less time and resources on marketing simply because they have invested their time, energy and resources in creating a quality brand. In other words, the brand sells itself. Anyone who is in the market for a Bentley doesn't need to be convinced and sold on the quality of the product, because the quality speaks for itself.

When you are a single man or woman of quality and substance, you'll never have to advertise who you are because your quality will speak for itself. Those who are seeking quality relationships will find you, and those who are seeking quantity relationships will find everyone else. Never compromise your quality to attract the quantity. Be patient enough to wait on someone who can handle who you are spiritually, emotionally and physically. There are few things that are worse than something that is quality falling in the hands of someone who is not equipped to handle it correctly.

Many of you are wondering why God won't hurry up and deliver your quality mate. The truth is, you don't want anyone who isn't prepared to handle who you are as a quality individual. You are God's pride and joy, His private stock, and He loves you too much to place your heart in the hands of someone who doesn't know your worth. As much as I love my sons, I know that there are certain blessings that I can't give them until they are mature enough to handle them. My prayer is that you will be patient enough to allow God to prepare and present that quality mate in His perfect timing and not yours. When we allow God to put it together, the devil can't tear it apart.

Conclusion

I can remember it like it was just yesterday. I would spend Sunday afternoons driving around town with mom after church as she delivered homemade meals that she had prepared to a few of the elderly people from the church. It seemed like no matter whose house it was that we entered into, it was always the same scene. Every one of those adorable elderly people had that one room in their home where nobody was ever allowed to sit in. It was almost like an exhibit in a museum. The furniture was covered in plastic, the carpet always had fresh vacuum lines in it, and the porcelain figurines were on display in the china cabinet. You just knew not to enter into that room, and you certainly know not to touch anything in that room.

The reason you didn't go into that room was because it was reserved for special guests and for special occasions. It was not reserved for those who just "stopped by". Did you know that God loves you so much that He has chosen to set you aside for a special person, and a special occasion? God never intended for your heart to be the place where people pop up and hang out. You are God's best kept secret, and His private selection. He has set you aside for the right person who is mature enough to recognize your worth, and who is caring enough to handle you without damaging you.

What I hope that you have taken away from this book is the reality that you are someone special designed for someone special. God had amazing things in mind when He created you, and His desire for you is to take you back to the Garden of Eden: the place where you were set aside to relish in the joy and the peace that was intended for you at creation. I hope that you are walking away with a sense of peace knowing that because you are God's best, He certainly has His best in store for you in every area of your life, including your relationships. I wish you nothing but God's very best in life, love and leadership as you forge forward in the things of God.

Made in the USA
Monee, IL
02 March 2023